Exploring
Fire Tablet

Kevin Wilson

Exploring Fire Tablets

Publisher: Elluminet Press
Director: Kevin Wilson
Lead Editor: Steven Ashmore
Technical Reviewer: Mike Taylor, Robert Ashcroft
Copy Editors: Joanne Taylor, James Marsh
Proof Reader: Mike Taylor
Indexer: James Marsh
Cover Designer: Kevin Wilson

eBook versions and licenses are also available for most titles. Any source code or other supplementary materials referenced by the author in this text is available to readers at

www.elluminetpress.com/resources

For detailed information about how to locate your book's resources, go to

www.elluminetpress.com/resources

Table of Contents

About the Author

With over 15 years' experience in the computer industry, Kevin Wilson has made a career out of technology and showing others how to use it. After earning a master's degree in computer science, software engineering, and multimedia systems, Kevin has held various positions in the IT industry including graphic & web design, building & managing corporate networks, training, and IT support.

He currently serves as Elluminet Press Ltd's senior writer and director, he periodically teaches computer science at college in South Africa and serves as an IT trainer in England. His books have become a valuable resource among the students in England, South Africa and our partners in the United States.

Kevin's motto is clear: "If you can't explain something simply, then you haven't understood it well enough." To that end, he has created the Exploring Technology Series, in which he breaks down complex technological subjects into smaller, easy-to-follow steps that students and ordinary computer users can put into practice.

Acknowledgements

Thanks to all the staff at Luminescent Media & Elluminet Press for their passion, dedication and hard work in the preparation and production of this book.

To all my friends and family for their continued support and encouragement in all my writing projects.

To all my colleagues, students and testers who took the time to test procedures and offer feedback on the book

Finally thanks to you the reader for choosing this book. I hope it helps you to use your Fire Tablet with greater understanding.

Have fun!

Fire Tablets

Formerly known as the Kindle Fire, the Fire Tablet is a touch screen device developed by Amazon and is based on the Android Operating System.

The Fire Tablet comes with its own operating system called Fire OS, whose user interface is designed to promote Amazon's services, such as the Appstore, Amazon Video, Music, Prime, and Kindle ebook Store.

The Fire's home screen features recently accessed content and apps. Categories are provided for different types of content, such as ebooks, apps, games, music, magazines, and videos. These show up as a carousel menu at the top of the screen.

Lets take a look at the different models that are currently available.

Available Models

There are three versions currently available: Fire Tablet 7, Fire Tablet HD 8, and Fire Tablet HD 10.

Fire 7 features a 7" 1024 x 600 display, the Fire HD 8 has an 8" 1280 x 800 HD display, and the Fire HD 10's screen is a 10" 1920 x 1200 full HD display.

The Fire 7 & HD 8 both use micro USB 2.0 connectivity, so will include a micro USB 2.0 port on the bottom of the tablet. The HD 10 now uses a USB-C type port.

There is a choice between 16GB or 32GB of on board storage for the 7 & HD 8 models, and 32GB or 64GB for the HD 10. All models are expandable using a micro SD card.

All three models now include Amazon Alexa voice assistant.

There are also kids versions of the Fire Tablet available. The Fire 7 kids edition, Fire HD 8 kids edition and the fire HD 10 kids edition. These are more or less identical in hardware specs, with a few exceptions such as more rugged hardware with a two year warranty, and a 'kid proof' case, in case your child drops it or stands on it.

Features

Fire Tablets come with internal storage starting at 16GB and 32GB on the Fire 7 and Fire 8 HD. While on the Fire HD 10, you can have 32GB or 64GB. All these tablets are expandable using a microSD card you slot into the side of your tablet. This allows you to store more photos, movies, compatible apps and games.

All three models features a 2 mega pixel rear-facing camera for taking photos or recording 720p HD video.

You'll also find a front facing camera just above the screen that you can use for video chat.

You can choose from a whole library of Kindle eBook and magazine titles, as well as all your favourite movies and TV shows on Prime Video, Netflix, and popular local TV channels.

The app store allows you to download thousands of apps both paid and free such as Facebook, Twitter, Spotify, Candy Crush Saga, Subway Surfers, and so on.

Enjoy all the best songs from thousands of artists, using the Amazon Digital Music Store to download them to Your Music Library.

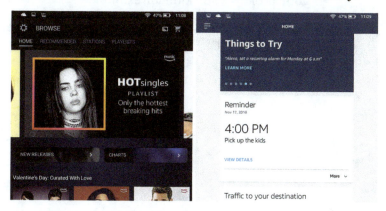

Amazon Alexa is Amazon's voice activated virtual assistant. Alexa provides quick access to the entertainment you want, including music, games, audiobooks, and eBooks. You can also ask Alexa questions about anything, check your calendar, skype, send messages, get news, sport, traffic updates, and so on.

Browse the internet with the silk web browser and check your email with the email app.

Setting up your Fire Tablet

Your Fire Tablet is pretty much ready to go out of the box, but there are a few things you should do before you get started.

In this chapter we'll go through the procedures on how to register your Fire Tablet with your Amazon Account, add email accounts, social media, as well as adding user profiles for different users who might use your tablet - your kids for example.

Lets take a look at setting up your Fire Tablet and getting started.

First Steps

Lets take a closer look at the Fire Tablet itself. If we have a look along the top edge of the tablet you'll see some buttons and ports.

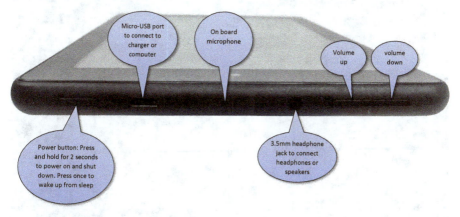

Here you'll find your power button, a micro USB port to connect to your charger or computer, volume control buttons, and a 1/8th inch (3.5mm) headphone jack for you to connect your headphones or external speakers.

You can also purchase adapters to plug into your micro USB port to transfer photos from a camera, memory card, or memory stick directly into the Prime Photos App.

Along the right hand edge, you'll find a micro SD card slot, where you can add some more storage space for offline music, photos or documents.

Chapter 2: Setting up your Fire Tablet

On the back of your tablet, you'll find your main camera on the top left.

There is also a front facing camera located just above your screen. This one comes in handy for selfies and video chats.

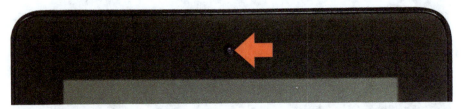

Before we do anything else, you should charge up your Fire Tablet using the charger that comes in the pack. Your Fire Tablet is shipped with about 40 to 50% charge. It's good practice to charge it up to 100% first before use. Also for best battery life, you should not allow the battery on your Fire Tablet to drain all the way down to 0%, try recharging at about 20% at a minimum.

Plug the micro USB cable into the port on the top of your Fire Tablet.

Plug the other end into the charger, then plug the charger into the wall and you're all set.

You can still get going and set up your Fire Tablet while it is plugged in and charging.

Initial Setup

When you first power up your Fire Tablet, you'll need to go through the initial setup phase. This registers your Fire Tablet with your amazon account, and connects to your wifi.

First go down to the 'choose your language' section in the middle of the screen. Tap the selection to choose your language from the list.

You can scroll up and down the list if you tap and drag your finger down the screen.

Tap the continue icon at the bottom right of the page.

Select your region. This will format dates and times correctly. Tap the continue icon at the bottom right of the page.

Now select your wifi network. If you are connecting at home, your wifi network and password is usually printed on the back of your router. If you can't find it, get in touch with your service provider. Select your network name in the list.

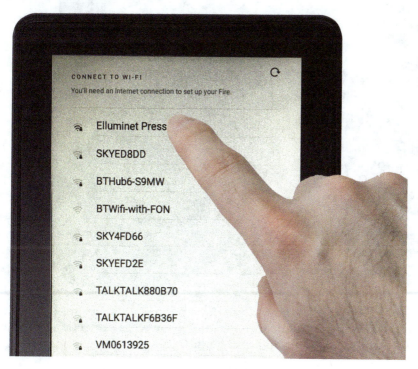

Chapter 2: Setting up your Fire Tablet

Enter your wifi password when prompted. Good practice is to enable the box 'hide password'. This masks your password so no one can see what you're typing in. Tap 'connect' when you're done.

Your Fire Tablet will now check for updates, this can take a while to complete, depending on the speed of your wifi connection. Your Fire Tablet will restart and install the updates.

Once the update is complete, you will need to register your Fire Tablet with your amazon account. All you need to do is enter the details and tap 'continue' on the bottom right of the screen.

Tap 'continue' when you're done.

If you have two-step authentication turned on, you'll need to enter the code sent as a text message to your phone. Enter the code then tap 'sign in'.

Tap 'update now' on the update screen if prompted.

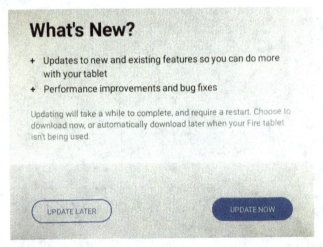

This will ensure you have the latest software installed on your fire tablet.

If you have bought a new Fire Tablet or restoring it for some reason, you can select a backup to restore all your apps and personal data. To do this select the latest backup then tap 'restore' at the bottom of the screen.

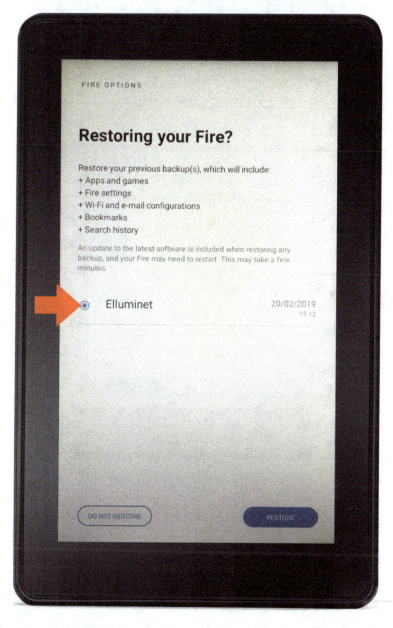

If you want a clean Fire Tablet and set it up as new, select 'do not restore'.

Chapter 2: Setting up your Fire Tablet

Select the 'fire options' you want to enable or disable. Tap the tick boxes next to the options to enable or disable them.

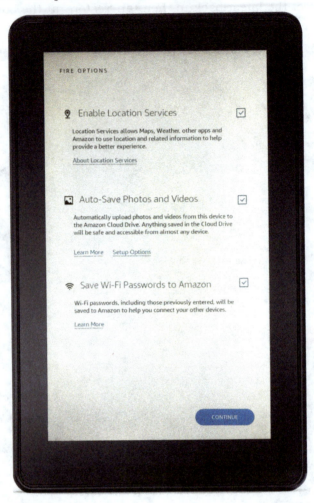

Location services allows your Fire Tablet to detect your approximate location and allows you to use apps that provide you with regional information, such as weather, traffic, local points of interest, places to eat, local news, and so on.

Personally I prefer not saving my wifi password to amazon.

It's a good idea to allow your Fire Tablet to automatically save any photos or videos you shoot with the on board camera.

Your Fire Tablet will back itself up to amazon's cloud storage; your email, configuration settings, entered passwords for your wifi or websites, downloaded music, tv programmes or films.

Setup Amazon Alexa. Tap 'continue' on the 'alexa on your fire' screen.

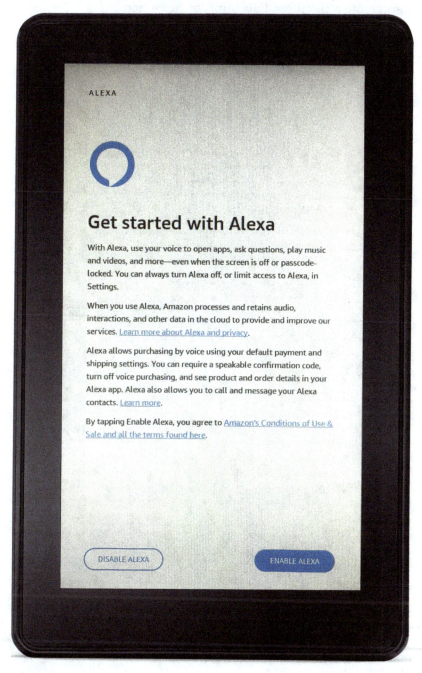

Tap 'enable alexa' on the bottom right of the screen to enable alexa. Tap 'finish' when you're done.

Chapter 2: Setting up your Fire Tablet

If you have any young children that are likely to use your Fire Tablet, you can create a monitored account for them here.

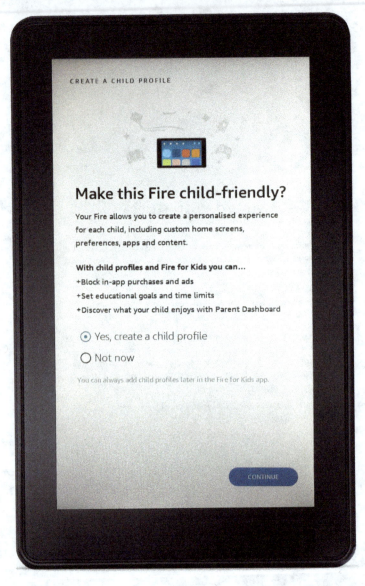

To set up a child account, tap 'yes' and follow the steps to enter their name and details.

If you don't want to create one now, tap 'not now'. You can always set one up later if you need to.

Tap 'continue' on the bottom right of the screen.

Tap 'connect' to add your 'goodreads' account.

If you don't use either of these, just tap 'continue' on the bottom right of the screen.

Configure your Amazon Prime Account. Note Amazon Prime is **not** a free service and costs £79 a year. If you sign up, you will get a free trial but you'll be charged after 30 days if you don't cancel.

If you order a lot of things from Amazon, you get free delivery with most orders, so it can benefit you depending on how you shop. Also you can stream tv shows, films, and music directly to your Fire Tablet. You can also lend books from the Fire Tablet lending library rather than buying them. So if you enjoy doing all that, then Amazon Prime is worth it. To sign up for your account 'tap start your 30-day free trial' or 'sign up and pay for Prime'.

If you're not interested in that just tap 'no thanks'.

Audio Books subscription. Select 'no thanks', unless you listen to a lot of audio books. In this case tap 'start my free trial' - note there is a subscription fee for this.

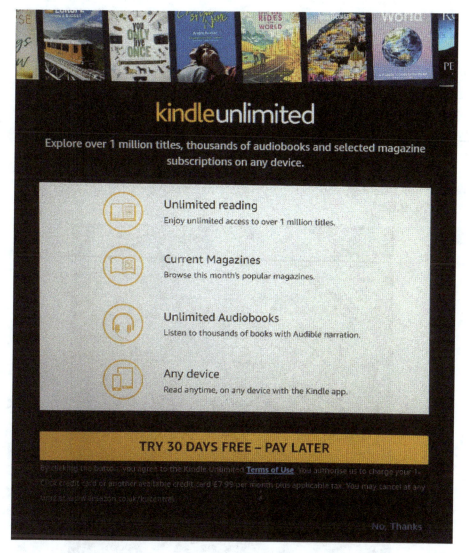

Tap 'continue' on the 'welcome tutorial'.

Take a look at the initial set up procedure video demo. Open your web browser and navigate to the following website

www.elluminetpress.com/using-fire-tablets

Setup your Email

The Fire Tablet includes an app that allows you to add your email accounts. You can add more than one, if you have them.

To add your email address, open up the email app from your home screen.

If this is the first time running the app, you will be prompted for your email address and password. Tap 'hide password', this just masks the password field so no one can see what you type in. Tap 'next' when you're done.

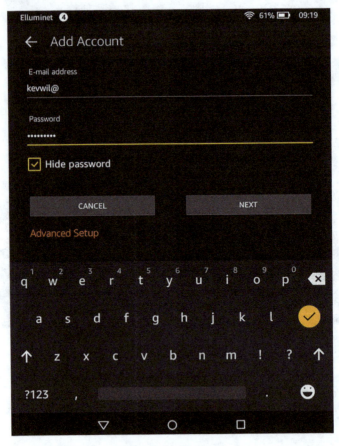

Now sign in with your email address and password, then tap 'next'.

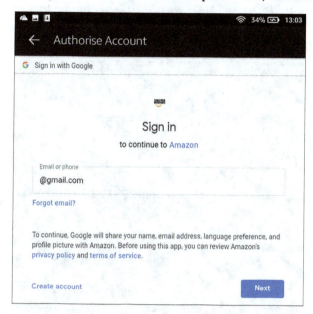

Allow amazon access to your email account

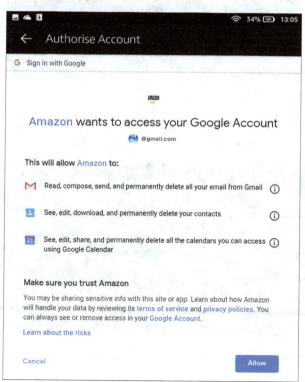

With some email addresses, you may be prompted for an account type. Most email providers use IMAP, so it's safe to choose this one. However, if you are adding your work, school or college email address, then these are usually Exchange accounts.

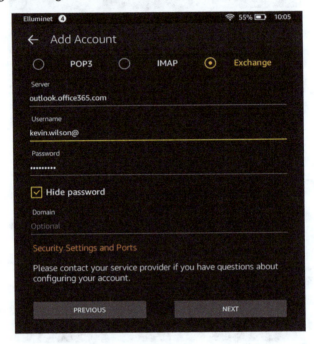

For Office 365 exchange accounts use the following server

`outlook.office365.com`

If you have more than one email address, tap 'add another account' and repeat the process to add your other addresses.

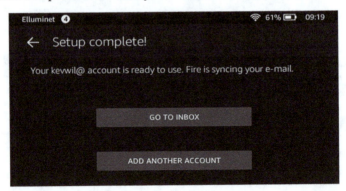

If this is your only email address, tap 'go to inbox'. The app will take you to your inbox.

You can get back to the email settings to add other accounts at a later date. To do this, in the email app open the sidebar

Select 'add account'.

Go through same procedure as before.

Social Media

You can add your social media accounts for goodreads, facebook, twitter, instagram and so on. You can add goodreads from the settings app, for the others you'll need to download the app.

To add goodreads, swipe down with your finger from the top edge of the screen.

Select the 'settings' icon.

Tap 'my account'

Select 'social networks'.

To connect to your goodreads account, tap 'connect' next to 'connect to goodreads'.

If you have a goodreads account, tap 'connect existing account' and enter your goodreads email address and password. Tap 'sign in'.

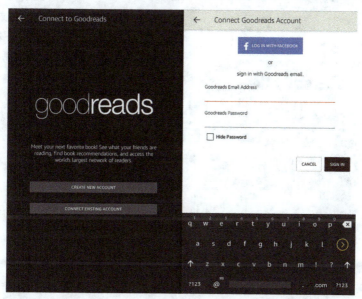

If you don't have one, click 'create new account' and amazon will create one for your.

Other Social Networks

To add any others such as twitter facebook, instagram or snapchat, you'll need to search for and download the apps from the app store.

Tap the search icon on the top right, then type in the app you want to install. In this example 'facebook'. From the drop down suggestions tap 'download' next to the app you want.

Once installed, you'll find the app on your home screen. Tap on the icon to start the app. You might need to scroll up to see the next page of apps if you don't see it.

Once the app opens, tap 'log in'.

Enter your facebook username and password

Tap 'log in'.

Now you can browse through your facebook feed, share photos, post updates and so on, as you would normally do.

Follow the same procedure to install instagram, twitter, and any other social network you use.

Adding Profiles

The Fire Tablet allows you to create profiles for other users who may use your tablet. This ensures privacy and security, and allows the users to get a personalised account when they use the Fire Tablet. It also allows you to set up monitored and restricted profiles for your children to help protect them online and to keep a track of what they're doing while using your Fire Tablet.

Adult Profile

Swipe down with your finger from the top edge of the screen and select 'settings'. Tap 'profiles & family library'.

To add another adult profile, tap 'add a second adult profile'.

Sign in with your amazon account password.

Pass the tablet to the person you're adding and ask them to sign in with their amazon account email and password.

Choose the data you want to share within 'the family'. A good idea is not to share payment information and allow each person to use their own, so select 'we do not want to share payment methods and only agree to share management of child profiles across amazon devices.'

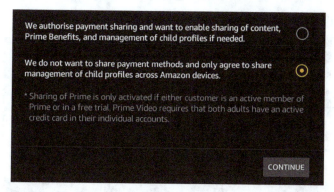

To switch user, you can swipe down from the top edge of the screen and tap the profile icon on the top right. Select the profile from the selections.

You can also select from the lock screen. Tap the profile icon on the top right of the screen, and from the drop down, select your profile

Child Profile

Swipe down with your finger from the top edge of your screen and select 'settings'.

Tap 'profiles & family library' then select 'add a child profile

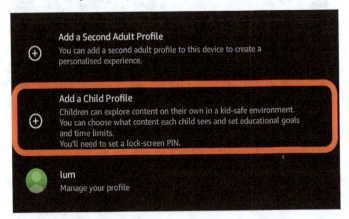

Enter the child's name, date of birth.

Tap 'add profile' when you're finished.

Managing Child Profiles

To access the profiles you've set up for your kids, swipe down from the top edge of the screen and tap 'settings'. Scroll down the list and tap 'profiles & family library'.

At the bottom of the screen, you'll see a list of profiles that have been set up. In this example, I'm going to go through the settings on Sophie's profile.

Set bedtimes when kindle is locked, usage time limits. Set targets for reading books, videos, or apps.

Set your child's age range so your kindle filters out content not appropriate for this age group.

Restrict books, videos, and apps. Allows you to add only the content you want your child to use

Paid Subscription that allows you to add age appropriate books, apps and videos for your children

Scroll down the page to reveal the rest of the settings...

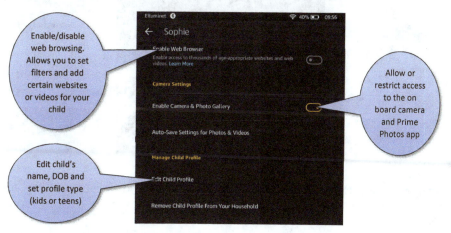

Enable/disable web browsing. Allows you to set filters and add certain websites or videos for your child

Allow or restrict access to the on board camera and Prime Photos app

Edit child's name, DOB and set profile type (kids or teens)

Setting Time Limits

To access the profiles you've set up for your kids, swipe down from the top edge of the screen and tap 'settings'. Scroll down the list and tap 'profiles & family library'.

On your child's profile, tap 'set daily goals & time limits'.

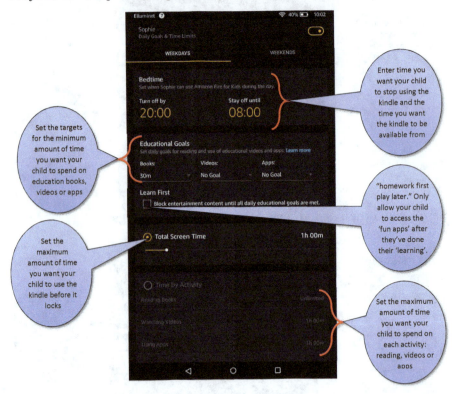

You can set these for weekdays and have a different setting for weekends. Use the two tabs 'weekdays' and 'weekends' on the top of the screen.

Parental Controls

Swipe down from the top edge of your Fire Tablet and tap 'settings'. Then select 'parental controls'. If it's your first time using parental controls, you'll need to turn the feature on.

To do this, slide the slider on the right hand side to 'on'. You'll be prompted to create a password.

Note that this enables the parental controls on the currently signed in profile and not the child's profile you created in the previous section.

Once you enable parental controls, you'll see a list of settings you can apply to your child's account.

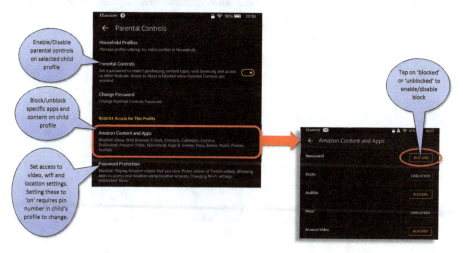

You can block/unblock certain apps and content

You can also block access to the Amazon stores and prevent purchases as well as monitor your child's activity. Tap the orange switches to turn on/off these features.

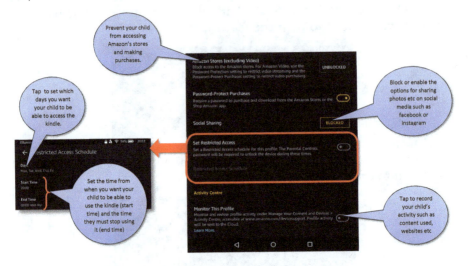

To view reports of your child's activity go to

www.amazon.com/mycd

Enter your amazon account email address and password. Tap 'your devices', then tap the device your child is using.

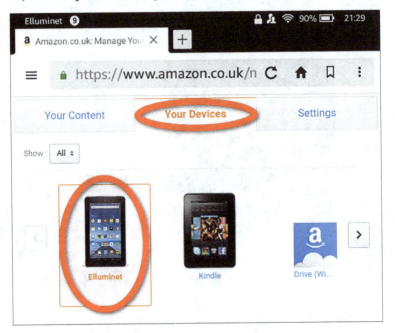

Scroll down the page and you'll see an activity centre. Here you can see the activity logs for your child.

Tap on 'web' to see the websites that your child has visited. Tap on the domain names in the list to open up the web pages.

You can do the same for apps, games, books, and so on

Configure Alexa

Alexa will pretty much work without any configuration. However there are a few things worth tweaking.

Tap the settings icon on the top left of the screen.

From the options, tap 'settings'.

Here, you can customise Alexa.

Chapter 2: Setting up your Fire Tablet

Your profile. Change your name, add voice profile of your voice so Alexa can recognise you.

Account Settings. View recognised voices and voice profiles, add kid skills. Kid skills are voice activated alexa apps that are designed for children. You can also turn on voice purchasing meaning you can ask alexa to order a product. If you do this, you should create a passcode you'll use to confirm any voice purchases. Tap 'alexa account', then 'voice purchasing'. Tap 'voice code' and enter a pin. You can also enable/disable voice responses and amazon household.

Device Settings. Here, you can add other amazon devices, such as the amazon echo or fire stick.

Notifications. Manage notification settings for Alexa's features.

Your Locations. Add your home address, work address and the addresses of any other places your visit regularly. This helps Alexa formulate traffic reports, weather and trigger reminders when you arrive at certain places.

Alexa Privacy. View and manage the data Alexa collects about you, as well as alexa skill permissions, device history and voice history.

Communication. Link communication apps to Alexa, eg add skype.

Music. Add music services, eg spotify. Tap 'link new service', tap 'spotify' then enter your spotify email address and password.

TV & Video. Add TV and video streaming services, eg fire tv. Tap the app. Tap 'link your alexa device'.

Flash Briefing. This is your news updates. Tap 'add content', then select your news network, eg BBC News, CNN, etc

Traffic. Tap 'traffic'. In the 'to' field, enter the streetname and postcode/ zipcode of the location you want a traffic update to. Eg your work address.

Sports updates. Tap 'sports', then tap 'add team'. Type in the name of your team. Tap the team name in the search results, then tap 'save'.

Calendar. Tap 'calendars', then select which account you have - GMail, Microsoft Account, or Apple iCloud. Tap 'continue', then enter your email address and password.

Lists. Create shopping lists and to-do lists.

Add a Pass Code

To make your Fire Tablet secure, you can add a pass code. To do this, tap the settings app on your home screen

Scroll down and tap 'security & privacy'.

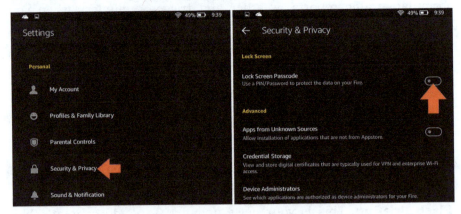

Enter a 4 digit passcode into the fields, then tap 'finish'.

Now whenever you unlock your fire tablet, you'll be prompted for the pass code.

The Amazon Cloud

Content purchased from Amazon is securely stored remotely on one of Amazon's servers and is known as the cloud. The idea is to allow you to access your content from anywhere not just on your home computer or Fire Tablet.

Cloud Storage

All your music, books, newspapers, purchased videos, films and apps are stored on the cloud and are synced, copied or streamed to your Fire Tablet as and when you access them.

As you can see from the illustration above, Amazon's online store, the music store, app store, kindle store and Amazon Prime are all located in the cloud servers, similar to the ones below.

Very little is stored locally on your Fire Tablet. This means for your Fire Tablet to function properly, it needs a constant connection to the internet to do so.

Uploading Photos from your PC

On your PC open your web browser and navigate to

`www.amazon.com/gp/drive/app-download`

Click 'download the app', then from the prompt that appears, click 'run', or double click the download on the bottom left.

From the 'welcome to amazon drive' window, click 'install'.

Enter your amazon account email address and password when prompted. Click 'sign in'.

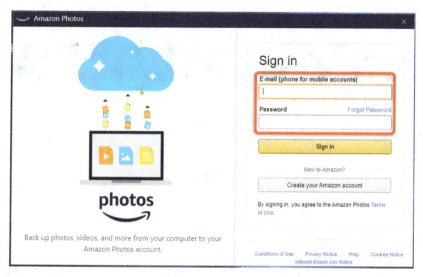

Click 'start backup'. This will backup all your photos and videos you have on your PC to the Amazon cloud.

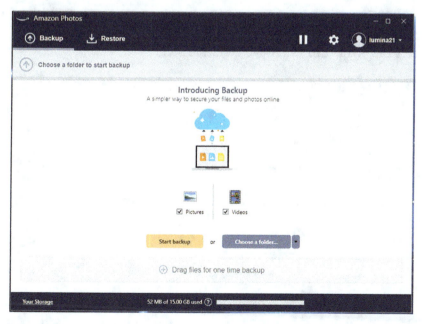

If you have photos or videos in any other folder, click 'choose a folder', then select the folder they're saved in.

You'll be able to view these photos on your Fire Tablet.

Using Amazon Cloud Drive

Download and install the Amazon photos app as demonstrated in the previous section.

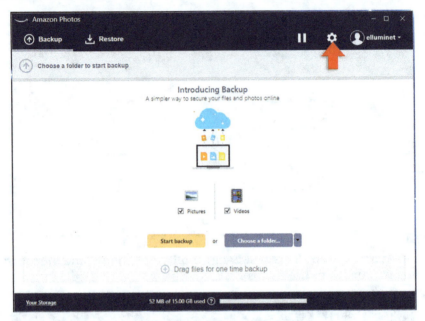

Select the 'sync' tab, then click 'enable sync'

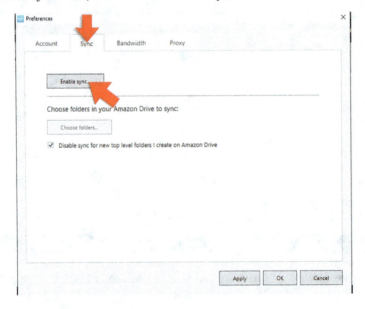

Click 'yes' on the confirmation dialog box.

Click 'choose folders'.

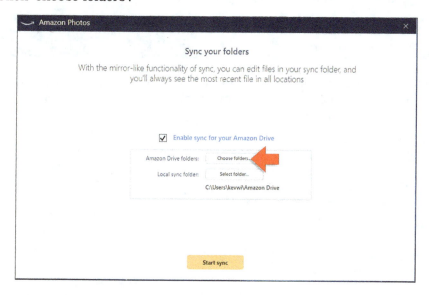

From the popup window, select the folders you want to sync to your Fire Tablet. Click 'ok'.

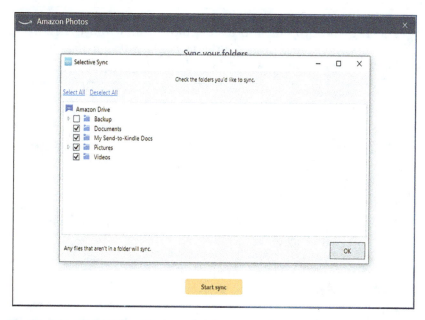

Click 'start sync'

Any files in the folders you selected will by synchronised to Amazon Drive. You'll be able to see these files on your Fire Tablet or any amazon device.

Chapter 2: Setting up your Fire Tablet

On your PC, open file explorer.

On the left hand side of the window, you'll see a new section called 'amazon drive'. Click on this icon to show your files on your cloud drive. As shown below.

You can drag and drop files in to the folders shown in the right hand pane. In this example, I am moving a PDF document I downloaded. This document is in the downloads folder.

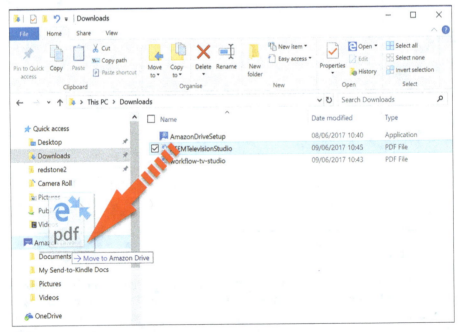

These files will be copied to your Fire Tablet. Select 'home' from the carousel menu along the top of your screen.

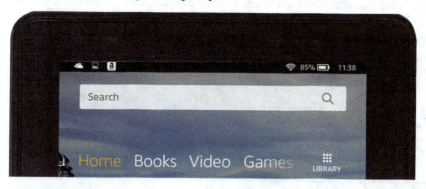

Tap the 'docs' app from the icons...

Chapter 2: Setting up your Fire Tablet

From the options along the top, tap 'cloud drive'.

You'll see the documents you've synced to your cloud drive. Any file you drag to the amazon drive folder in file explorer on your PC will be shown here.

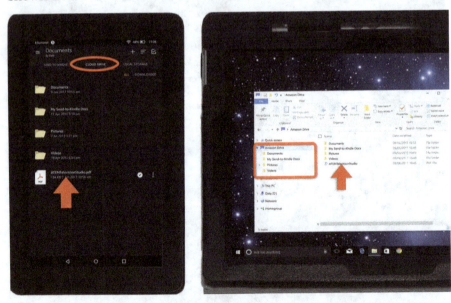

Tap on the file on your Fire Tablet to open it up.

Adding an SD Card

You can expand the internal memory with a micro SD card such as the one shown below. You can currently use up to 256GB microSD cards.

For best results, use Class 10 or equivalent high speed micro SD cards for optimal performance. Cards of this type will have any of these markings on...

To insert the card, turn your Fire Tablet off, then open the protective cover on the side and insert the card until it clicks in place.

Close the cover and power on your Fire Tablet.

Chapter 2: Setting up your Fire Tablet

Now, on your Fire Tablet, open up the settings app on your home screen, then select 'storage'.

Tap 'erase SD card'. This will wipe the card and format it for the Fire Tablet. Tap 'erase' on the confirmation dialog box.

Now, select the features you want your Fire Tablet to store on the SD card. Music, moves, photos, audiobooks and ebooks are good ones to move over. Click the switch icons to turn then on and off.

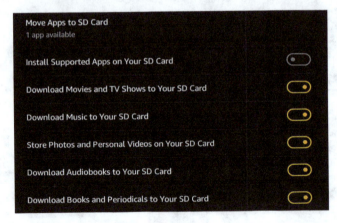

You can also install apps on the SD card, but the performance isn't as good as the card is slightly slower than the internal storoage. So I'd keep all the apps on internal storage.

To remove a card, first tap 'safely remove SD card' at the bottom of the storage settings, then press the card inwards first until it clicks. The card will pop out.

Pair a Bluetooth Device

First put the device into pairing mode. You'll need to refer to the device's instructions to find specific details on how to do this. On most devices, press and hold the pairing button until the status light starts flashing. This means the device is ready to be paired.

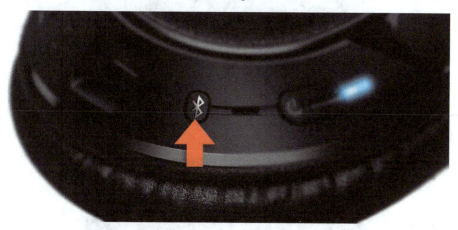

Open the settings app from the home screen on your Fire Tablet.

Chapter 2: Setting up your Fire Tablet

Tap 'wireless & bluetooth'

Tap 'bluetooth'.

Tap the switch next to 'bluetooth' to turn it on if it isn't already.

Then tap 'pair a bluetooth device'. Your Fire Tablet will now scan for nearby devices.

Once your Fire Tablet has found your device, tap on it in the list.

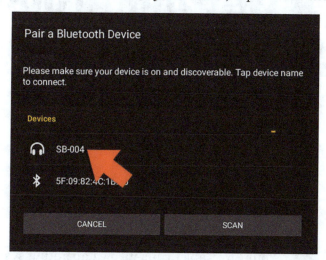

Your device will appear in the 'paired devices' list.

Getting Around Your Fire Tablet

Your Fire Tablet runs its own operating system called Fire OS which is a customized version of the android mobile operating system developed by Amazon.

Fire OS focuses on Amazon specific apps and services such as the silk web browser, Amazon's own email client, Amazon App Store, Prime Photos, Prime Video, Cloud Music Player, and Cloud Drive for storing documents, among other Apps available in the App Store.

Lets begin by taking a look at the Fire Tablet's home screen.

The Home Screen

First, lets take a look at the home screen. The home screen is divided into several sections highlighted in red below.

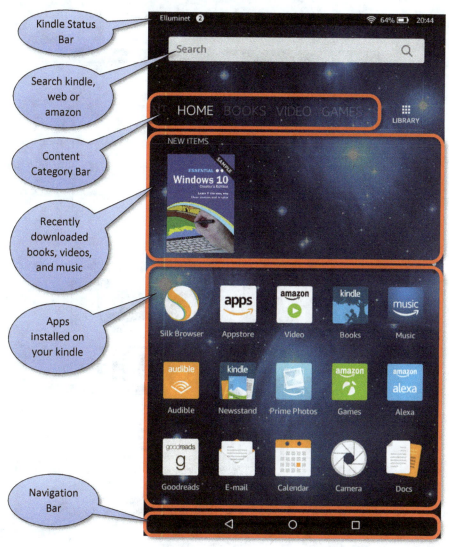

At the top of the screen you'll see a status bar. This shows the name of your tablet, wifi status, battery status, and the current time. Underneath that, you'll find a search field. This is where you can search the web, or the amazon store. Next is the carousel menu with different categories for content - books, videos, games, apps, etc. Swipe your finger left/right over the menu to scroll the categories - tap on one to switch to it.

Search Bar

The search bar allows you to search the web, the amazon store, and content you have purchased or downloaded.

You'll see the search results divided into three categories. The first is web which is a google web search.

With the web search you can search Google for websites as you would using a normal web browser. Just select 'web', then type your search keywords into the field at the top of the screen.

The next one across, is an Amazon Store search. Here, you can search for products on Amazon and buy them directly from your Fire Tablet.

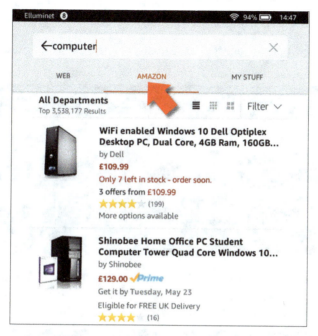

The last tab, allows you to search books, movies, and apps you have downloaded to your Fire Tablet.

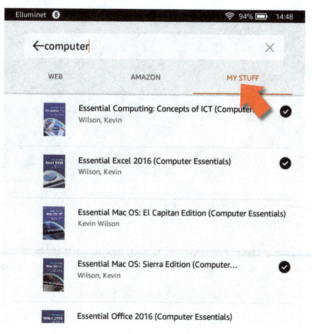

Categories Bar

Also known as the carousel menu, the categories bar allows you to see personalized content for each of the categories.

The category bar is located at the top of the screen, just under the search bar.

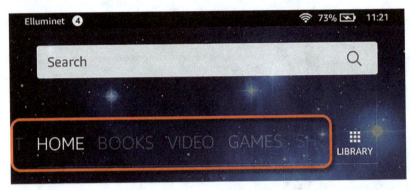

If you swipe across with your finger, you'll see 'Recent', 'Home', 'Books', 'Video', 'Games', 'Shop', 'Apps', 'Music', 'Audible', and 'Newsstand'. Tap on any of these to go to that category

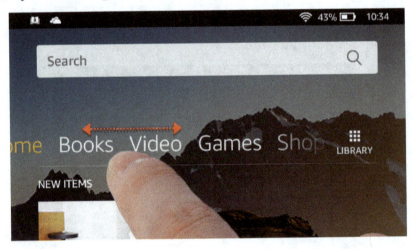

In each category you'll see the content Amazon recommends according to your browsing habits.

I find launching the relevant app from the home screen is a much better way to use apps and content you've already purchased.

If you are buying new content, then use the categories on the category bar.

New Items Section

The new items section appears just below the category bar and displays recently downloaded kindle books and magazines

Every time you download a new kindle book or magazine, the most recent 4 will appear in this list.

Installed Apps Section

You can find all the apps installed on your Fire Tablet on this section of your home screen. Swipe your finger up and down to see the rest of your apps.

The Navigation Bar

The navigation bar is located at the bottom of your screen and consists of three icons.

Go back to previous screen. Use this when browsing the web, the app store, book store and most apps.

Home. This button returns you to your home screen. You can use this button to return to your home screen from any app. Note when you do this, the app will still be running in the background.

Task switcher. This button displays all your open apps, allowing you to close them or switch to them.

Swipe up and down to scroll through the list. Swipe left to right across the app to close it down, or tap on the app to switch to it.

Navigating

The Fire Tablet, like many other tablets, makes use of touch screen technology. You navigate around the system using your finger to tap on objects on the screen. You can also use various gestures to operate certain commands. Lets take a look...

Have a look at the navigation video demos. Open your web browser and navigate to the following website.

`www.elluminetpress.com/kindle-nav`

Tap

Use your index finger to tap on an object on the screen. You can tap on an icon to launch an app. This is equivalent to the left click on your mouse.

Tap and Hold

Tap and hold your finger on an object, such as a book or app for a couple of seconds. This is similar to your right click and will reveal a context menu.

Tap and Drag

Tap your finger on an object such as an app icon. Then without lifting your finger, drag the object across your screen sliding your finger across the glass.

Swipe

Swipe your finger across the glass to turn pages in kindle books. Swipe up and down to quickly scroll web pages and so on. Use a similar action to 'striking a match'.

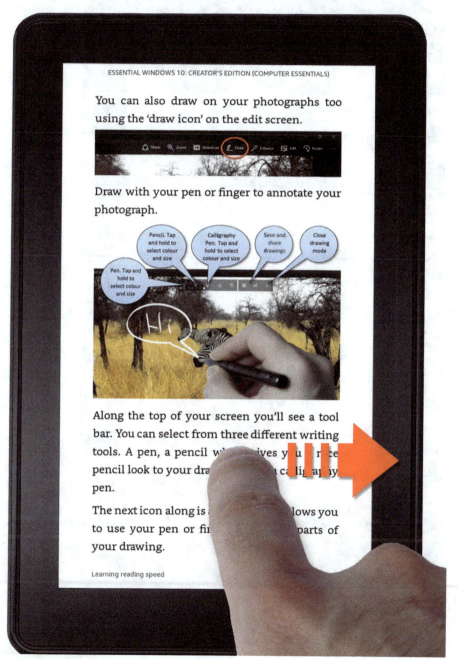

Scroll

Slide your finger up and down to scroll through a list of photographs, a website, your list of app icons, music, and so on.

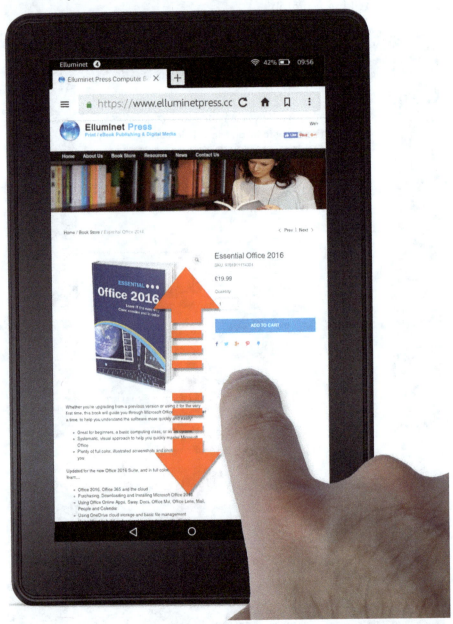

You can also slide your finger left and right across the screen to scroll sideways in some apps.

Swipe from Top Edge of Screen

Reveals your command centre, where you can find settings, wifi, screen brightness, screen rotation lock and so on.

To reveal the command centre, swipe your finger down from the top edge of the screen.

Swipe from Left Edge of Screen

Swiping in from the left edge of your screen reveals your app sidebar menu. Here you can adjust settings and functions specific to the app you are running at the time.

The Settings Menu

To reveal your settings menu, swipe down from the top edge of your screen.

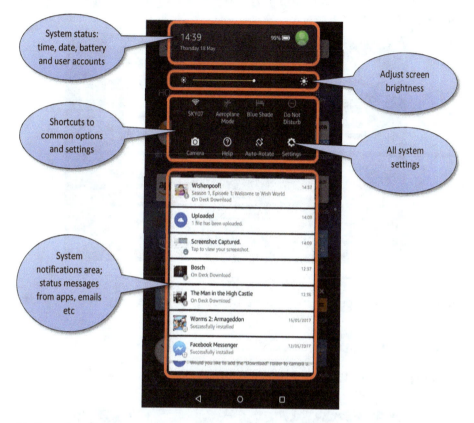

At the top of the menu, you'll see the current date and time, and to the right, you'll see your battery status and your user account icon. You can also use this icon to add additional users or switch to another user.

Underneath you'll see your screen brightness adjustment slider, tap and drag the slider left and right to change the brightness of your screen.

Under that you'll see your shortcuts to common settings and options. Here you can configure your wifi, access your camera, and open your system settings to make changes to preferences, and so on.

At the bottom, you'll see a list of all the notifications that have come in from apps such as downloads, updates and email notifications. You can tap on these notifications to go to the app or message.

Arranging Apps on Home Screen

You can move group or remove apps on your home screen. This helps to keep things together and tidy, so you can find the app you want quickly and easily.

I try to keep all my apps together. So for example, my email, contacts and calendar apps are next to each other as well as my web browser.

Move an App

To move an app, tap and hold your finger on the app icon for a second, then drag the app to the position you want to place it.

Grouping Apps

To create a group, tap and hold your finger on an app for a second, then drag the app and drop it on top of another. A useful tip is to group apps that are similar. So for example, email, calendar, and contacts could go in one group.

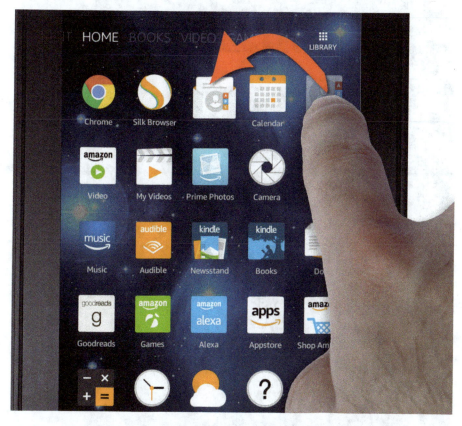

Here you can see a group has been created containing the email app and the contacts app. Just tap on the group to open it up.

Removing Apps

To remove an app, tap and hold your finger on the icon for a second then release your finger. You'll see a menu bar appear along the top of the screen. Tap 'uninstall' to remove the app.

Note you can't remove the pre-installed apps that come with your Fire Tablet.

Ask Alexa

Alexa is a digital personal assistant developed by Amazon and is capable of responding to voice commands, answering questions, playing music, making to-do lists, setting alarms, streaming podcasts, playing audiobooks, as well as weather, traffic, news, and other real time information.

If you have one of the newer Fire Tablets, you can talk to Alexa. To activate Alexa, hold down the home button until you see the blue bar appear. You can also say "Alexa!.

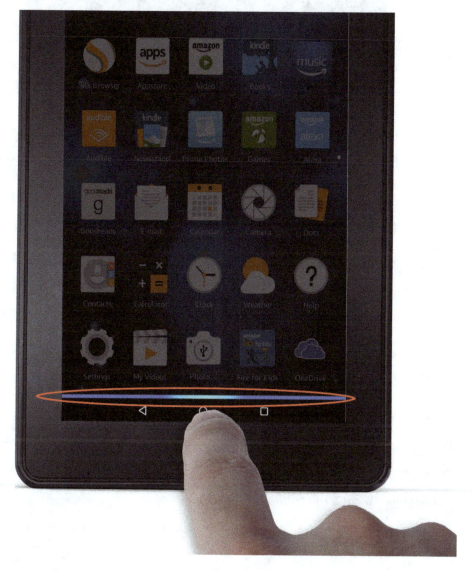

Then tell her what you need or ask her a question. Try a reminder....
"Remind me to pick up Claire at 4:30pm today."

Here are a few other commands to try.

Try saying: "What is the weather like tomorrow"

Try saying: "Find me a website on baking a cake"

Try saying: "What's the traffic like"

The more you use Alexa, the better she will understand you and will grow accustomed to your voice.

You can open the Alexa App from your home screen.

Here on the home page, you can see a list of all the things you've asked Alexa. You can scroll up and down these and tap on them to see details.

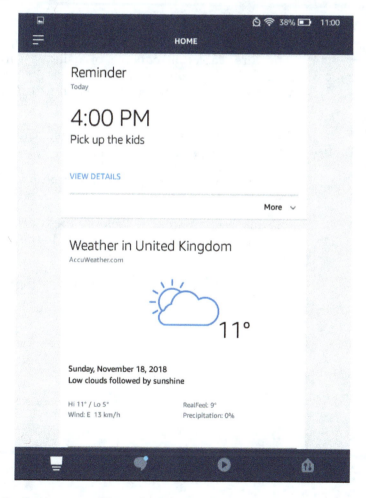

Along the bottom, you'll see four icons

Internet, Email & Communication

Your Fire Tablet is capable of using a variety of communication apps. You can browse the web with Amazon Silk, send and receive email with Amazon's Email Client.

You can also video skype friends, family, and colleagues using the Skype App.

Lets begin by taking a look around Amazon Silk Web Browser.

For this section take a look at the video demos. Open your web browser and navigate to the following website

www.elluminetpress.com/kindle-comms

Browsing the Web

On the Fire Tablet, you browse the web using a web browser called Silk. To launch silk, tap the icon on your home screen.

Once Silk opens, you'll come to the main screen.

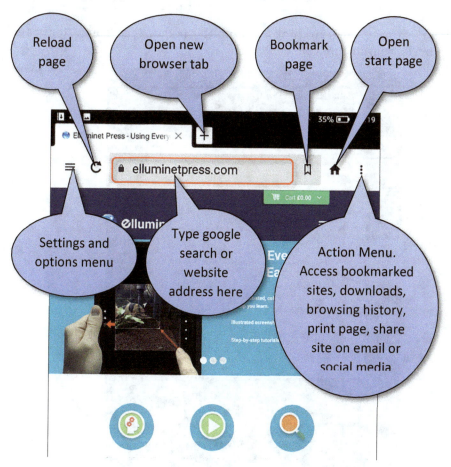

Along the top of your screen you'll see your navigation bar. Here you can type in a google search or the website address if you know it.

You can also bookmark your favourite sites, so you don't have to keep searching for them or remember the web address.

Google Search

You can navigate to any website using the 'search the web' field at the top of the screen. You can also type in a web address or URL if you have it.

If for example, I'm searching for computer books, type 'computer books' into the 'search the web' field.

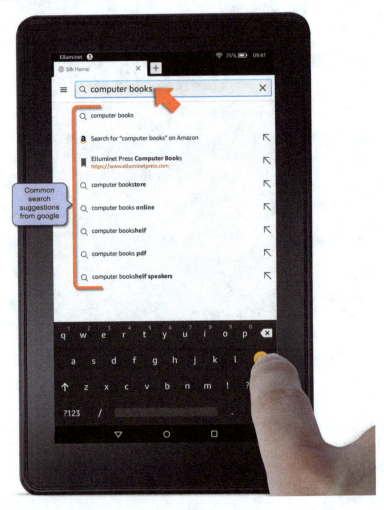

Settings & Options Sidebar

Swipe from left edge of your screen to reveal the options bar.

From here you can enter 'private browsing'. This prevents Silk from keeping a history of the websites you visit.

You can access your bookmarked sites and your reading list. You can see your website browsing history and your amazon lists such as your wish list.

You can also see a list of downloaded files you have downloaded using Silk.

You'll also find your settings menu.

Actions Menu

Tap the icon that looks like 3 dots. This will open up a sidebar on the right hand side of your screen.

Here, you can access your bookmarked sites, reading list, website browsing history, downloads folder and print out a webpage.

You can also share the current page you're looking at, search and go back to your start page.

Have a look at the illustration below.

Bookmarking Sites

Bookmarking sites is fairly simple. Navigate to the site you want and tap the bookmark icon at the top right of the screen. This will add the current site to your bookmarks list.

Select 'add bookmark' from popup menu.

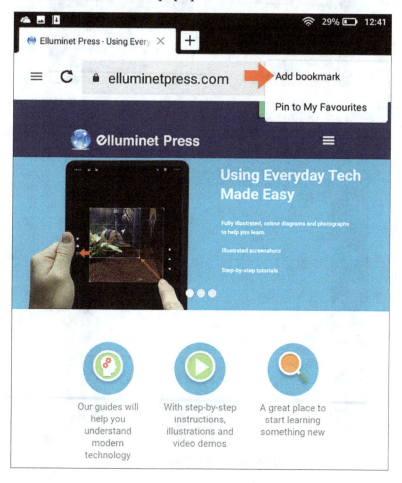

Revisit Bookmarked Site

To find your bookmarked sites, swipe from the left edge of the screen to reveal the sidebar. From the sidebar, tap on 'bookmarks'.

From the bookmarks page, you'll see the site you just bookmarked appear on the end of the list

Tap on the site name to go back to that site.

Organising Bookmarks

If you have a lot of bookmarked sites, you can create folders. First open the bookmarks page. To do this, tap the three dots icon on the top right.

From the side panel, tap 'bookmarks'.

Select 'view bookmarks' from the popup menu.

To create folders, on your bookmarks page, tap the second three dots icon, then select 'new folder'.

Give the folder a meaningful name, eg 'Media'. Type the name into the 'folder name' field. Then tap 'create'.

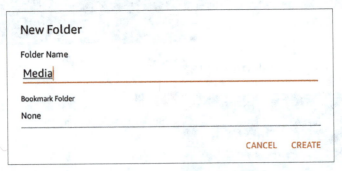

To move your bookmarks into a folder, tap the three dots icon next to the bookmark's name. Select 'edit' from the popup menu.

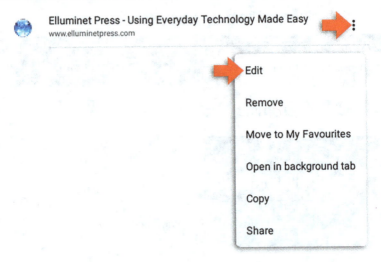

Tap in the 'bookmark name' field and select the folder.

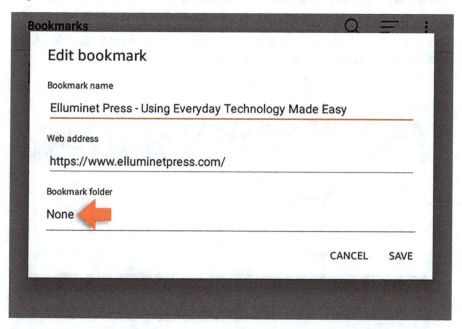

Select the folder to move your bookmark to, then tap 'select'.

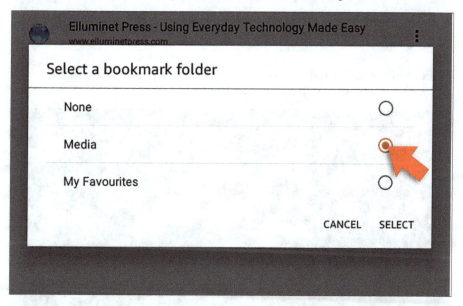

You can also edit, rename or remove web sites from your list. Tap the 3 dots icon next to the bookmark name, and select edit from the menu. You can type in a new bookmark name if needed.

Sharing Sites on Social Media

You can share sites on your social media time lines using the 'share' icon built into the silk browser. First you'll need to add your facebook and twitter accounts to your Fire Tablet.

To share the current site you are viewing, tap the action menu icon on the top right of the screen.

From the slide out menu, tap the 'share' icon, on the right hand side.

Select your social media network. In this case I am using facebook. If you use twitter, tap 'twitter' instead.

Sign into your social media account if prompted.

Now enter a comment to go with your post. Facebook will scan the website and select the main image to go with your post.

Tap 'post' to post to your time line.

Downloads

Whenever you download something from a website using Silk, you'll find it in your downloads folder.

To open your downloads folder, swipe from the left edge of the screen and tap 'downloads'.

To open any of the downloads, tap on the name in the list.

Browsing History

You can find your browsing history on the sidebar. Swipe from the left edge of the screen and tap 'history'.

From here you can see a list of all the sites you have visited. To revisit the site, just tap on the name in the list. To delete the site, tap the X on the right hand side.

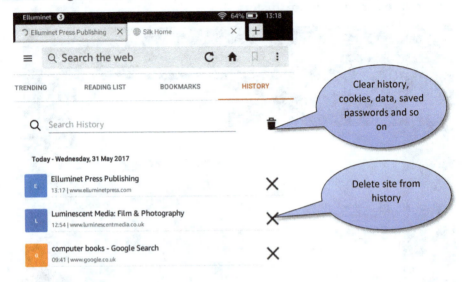

You can also clear your whole history, including visited websites, cookies, cached data, saved passwords.

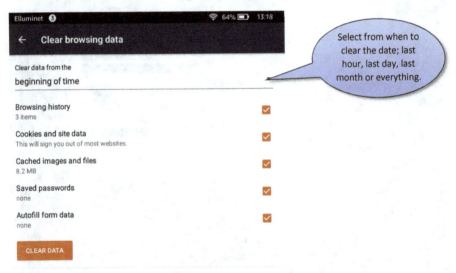

It's a good idea to clear this data once a month, as it removes cookies and other data some websites save to your device. Select everything in the list except 'saved passwords'. If you save your passwords for different websites you use, you'll have to enter them all again - so don't clear them.

Google Chrome

At the time of writing, Google Chrome Browser is not available in the Amazon App Store.

You can still install this app on your Fire Tablet, but first you need to disable 'apps from unknown sources' in your security settings.

Swipe down from the top edge of your screen. Go to settings -> security.

Set 'apps from unknown sources' to on, as shown below.

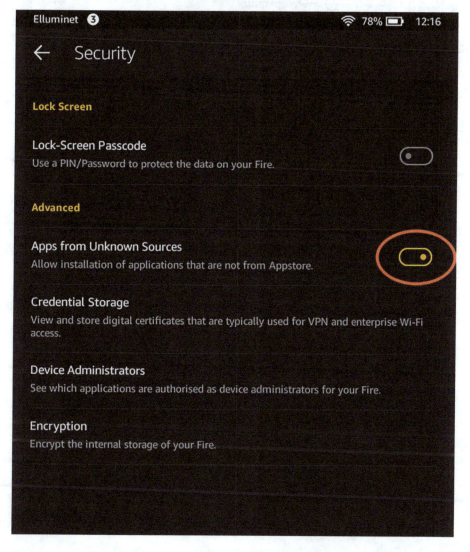

Be sure to turn this back on after you have installed Chrome.

Chapter 4: Internet, Email & Communication

You can download the Chrome package from

www.apkmirror.com/apk/google-inc/chrome/

Scroll down the page and find the latest version, then tap the download icon.

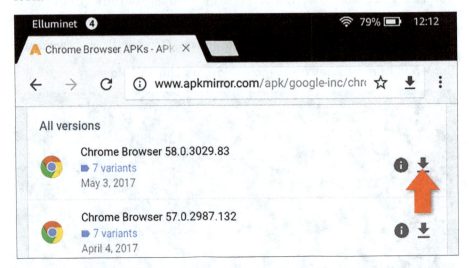

Scroll down the page and select the correct version for your Fire Tablet. The new Fire Tablets are based on Android 5 and use the ARM processor architecture. Tap the variant number to download.

Variant	Arch	Version	DPI
302908300 ❄ ∞ April 20, 2017	arm	Android 4.1+	nodpi
302908301 ❄ ∞ April 20, 2017	arm	Android 5.0+	nodpi
302908302 ❄ ∞ April 21, 2017	arm	Android 7.0+	nodpi
302908310 April 25, 2017	x86	Android 4.1+	nodpi
302908311 April 25, 2017	x86	Android 5.0+	nodpi

On the last page, scroll down until you see a blue button 'Download APK'. Tap on this button.

When prompted tap 'download' at the bottom of the screen. This will take a few seconds.

When the download is complete, tap 'open'. This will popup at the bottom of the screen when the download is complete.

Run through the installer, to install the package. The Google Chrome app will appear on your home page.

Make sure you disable 'apps from unknown sources' in your settings.

Using Email

Your Fire Tablet has a built in email app. You'll find this on your home screen

Once you launch the app, your email will open on the main screen. A list of all your emails will be listed. Just tap on one to read.

Tap the hamburger icon on the top left to change email account, if you have more than one set up. You can also access email settings, add additional email accounts, and change to a different mail folder such as inbox, outbox, drafts, trash, sent items, and so on.

To start a blank new email message, tap the blue pencil icon on the bottom right of the screen.

To delete email messages, swipe right to left over the message in the list.

To open emails in full, double tap on the message in the list.

Opening & Replying to Emails

To reply to an email, tap the email message you want from your inbox.

The email message will open in full screen. Here you can read your message, view any attachments and reply if you need to. In this particular email, there is an attachment.

Tap on the attachment thumbnail to open it up in full.

Tap the back arrow on the top left to go back to the message.

To reply to the message, tap the reply icon, circled below.

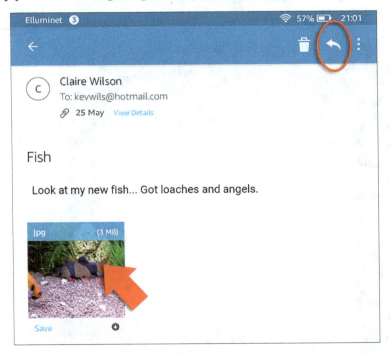

You can type in your message at the top, tap the send icon when you're done.

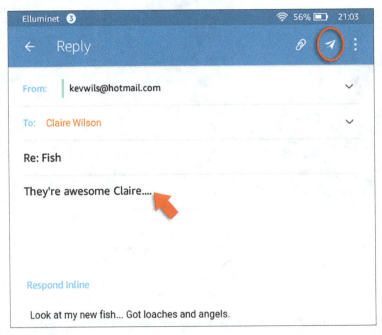

Sending a New Message

To send a new message, click the 'compose new email' icon on the bottom right of the screen.

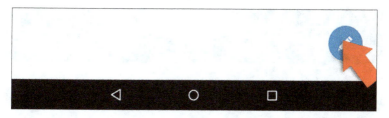

This will bring up a new email. Tap in the 'To:' field to enter an email address. If you are replying to a message, the email address of the person that sent you the message will appear here automatically.

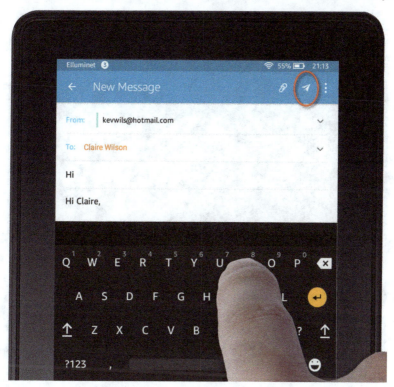

Tap in the subject field and add some text.

Tap in the message body underneath and type your message using the pop up on screen keyboard.

When you have finished, tap the send icon on the top right.

Adding an Attachment

To add an attachment to your email message, on your new message, tap on the paper clip icon.

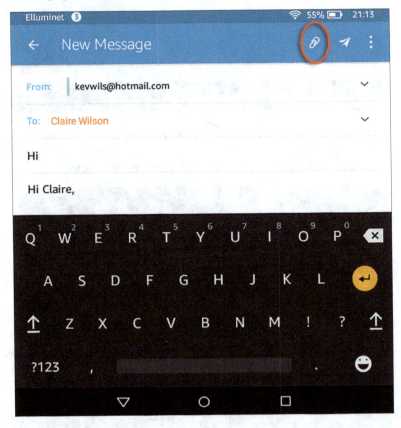

From the drop down menu you can choose to attach a photo you have already taken from your prime photos app, you can attach a file such as a document or PDF or you can take a photo using your camera.

In this example, I am going to attach a photo from the prime photos app.

From the prime photos app, select the photos you want to add. To add multiple photos, tap and hold your finger on the first photo you want, then tap the rest of the photos.

You'll see the photos appear at the bottom of your email message.

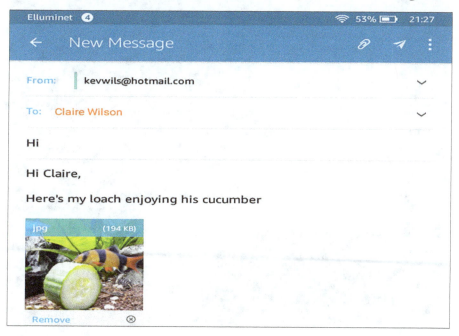

Deleting Messages

To delete messages, swipe your finger right to left over the message in your inbox.

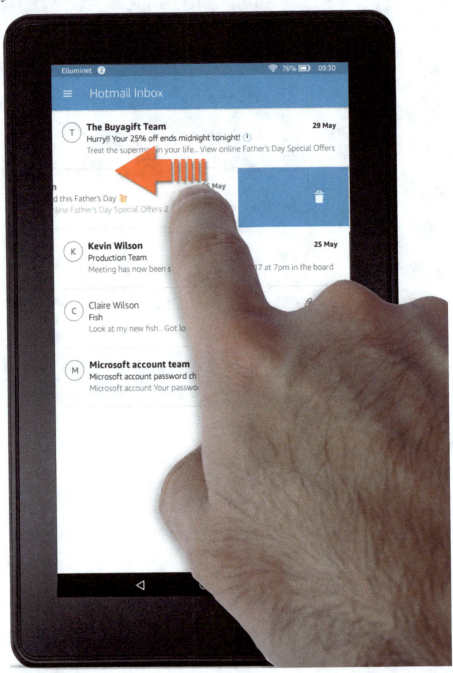

Email Folders

From the Email App, swipe your finger from the left edge of the screen to open the sidebar. You can also tap the hamburger icon on the top left of the screen.

You'll see your email accounts listed here. Tap on the email addresses to open the inbox for each account.

Tap on the small down arrow over on the right hand side of the panel to open the full list of folders for each account. Here, you'll find drafts, outbox, deleted and junk mail folders.

Skype

Skype is a video/chat app that allows you to send instant messages, make voice and video calls. Great for family living in other countries or friends that live a long way from you. Great way to keep in touch with people. Plus skype is free and more personal than a phone call or email.

From your home screen, tap on the Skype Icon. If you don't see the skype icon, go to the app store and download it.

Click 'sign in' at the bottom of the screen. You will need to sign in with a Microsoft account.

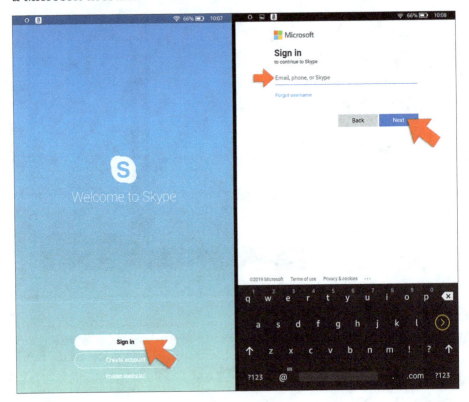

Tap 'next'.

Once you are in, give your friends your skype address so they can call you and have a video chat. This will be the email address you just signed in as.

When skype opens, you'll see the main screen. Lets take a look.

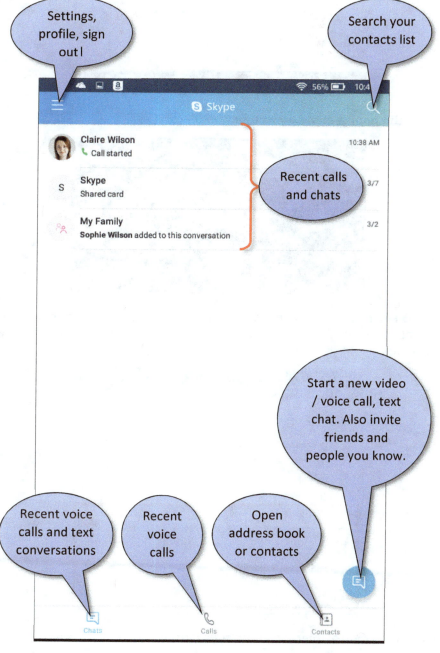

Making Video Calls

To make a new video call, select 'chats' from the three icons along the bottom of the screen, then tap the blue 'chat' icon on the bottom right hand corner.

From the popup menu, select 'new call'.

You'll see a list of people from your contacts list. If the person isn't there, you'll need to add them to your contact list. See adding new contacts.

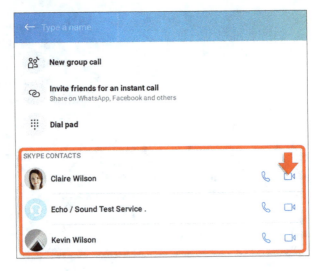

Click the small 'camera icon' on the right of the contact's name.

The Fire Tablet will display a preview of the front camera while waiting for the other person to answer. Make sure you're in the camera's frame.

Once the other person answers, your camera moves to the top right, and you'll see a shot of the person you're talking to on the main section of your screen, as you can see below.

Along the bottom of the screen you'll see a row of icons. If the icons along the bottom disappear, tap the screen once. Using these icons, you can mute your microphone or temporarily turn off your cam if you need to. You can also swap to the rear camera, which is useful if you want to show something - makes it easier than trying to turn your Fire Tablet around. Tap the red button to end the call.

Receiving Calls

When you receive an incoming call, you'll see this screen... The person's name will appear on the top left, and their profile photo will appear in the centre of the screen.

Tap the green camera icon on the bottom right to accept as a video call.

Tap the phone icon in the middle to accept as a voice call.

Tap the red icon on the left to decline the call.

Group Calls

You can invite multiple people to participate in a group chat. To do this, select 'chats' from the three icons along the bottom of the screen, then tap the blue 'chat' icon on the bottom right hand corner.

Select 'new group chat' from the popup menu.

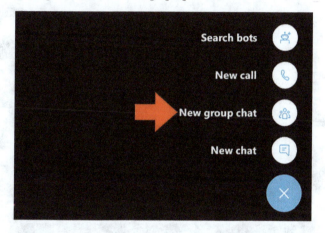

Select the people you want to invite to the chat from your contacts list.

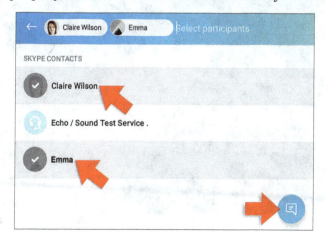

Tap the blue 'chat' icon on the bottom right.

Now, you can type in the field at the bottom of the screen to send the group a message. To start a video call to the group, tap the cam icon on the top right.

Wait for all members of the group to answer...

In this demo, Sophie is skyping Claire and her friend Emma. Lets take a look at the screen in a group conversation...

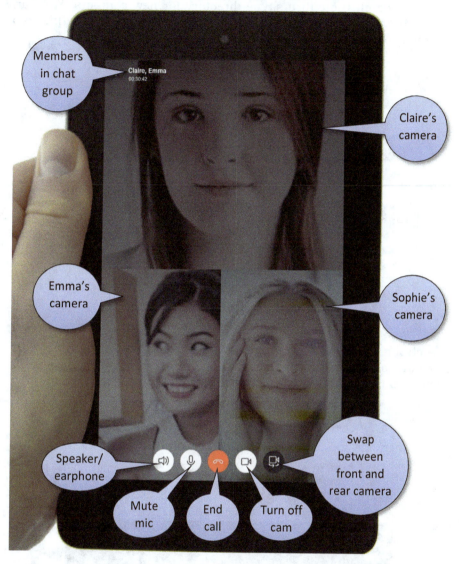

You'll usually see your camera on the bottom right, your other friends in the chat group will appear in their own tile on the main area of the screen.

On the top left, you'll see the names of the other contacts in the chat group.

To bring a person's chat tile to full screen double tap on it. Double tap again to return to normal view.

Adding Contacts

You can search the entire skype directory for new contacts. You can search by skype name, full name, or phone number. To do this, tap 'contacts' on the bottom right of the screen.

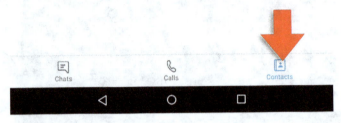

Tap 'add new contact' at the top

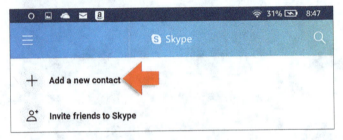

Search for the person you want to skype with. The best way to find someone is to use their email address. Most people on skype will have signed up using a Microsoft Account (eg hotmail.com or live.com).

Tap the name in the search results.

The skype chat window will open. Now from here, you can type in a text message using the field at the bottom, or start a video/voice chat using the camera or phone icons on the top right.

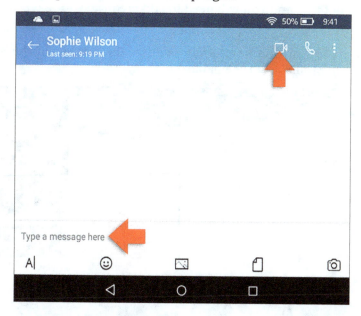

Tap the back arrow on the top left to return to your contacts list. You'll notice the name has been added to your 'skype contacts'.

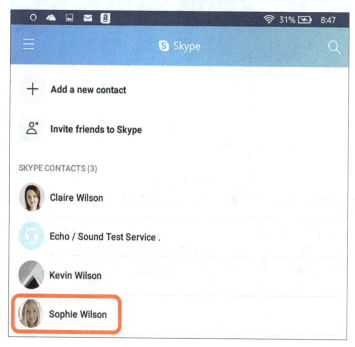

Making a Phone Call

You can make calls to a cell phone or a landline using skype. These calls are not free and you will need to add credit to your skype account to be able to do this.

To add credit, tap the hamburger icon on the top left of the screen, then select 'profile' from the sidebar.

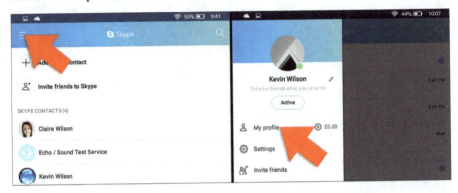

Tap 'add credit'

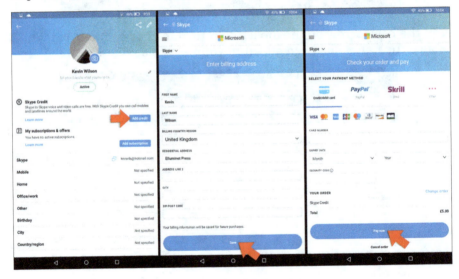

Enter your billing address, then tap 'save. Then select your payment method (eg credit card or paypal). Enter your card number, expiry date and other details. The default amount is £5, but if you need more credit, tap 'change order' then select an amount. Tap 'pay' at the bottom of the screen.

Tap the back arrow on the top left to go back to skype.

To make a phone call, tap the 'calls' icon on the bottom of the screen, then tap the keypad icon on the bottom left.

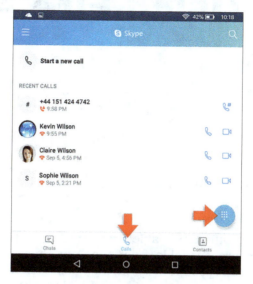

Key in the phone number using the keypad. Note, you'll need to use the international prefix to dial the numbers (+1 for US, +44 for UK).

Tap the phone icon at the bottom of the screen to place the call.

Using Fire Apps

Your Fire Tablet can run a variety of Apps that are available from the App Store. These Apps can be productivity apps such as word processors, email, messaging and video chat; or games and entertainment.

Some of these Apps are available for free but some you will need to pay for, the App store will tell you whether the App is free or not.

Lets begin by having a look around the App Store.

The App Store

The app store is where you'll purchase your apps and games. You can do this quite easily. To launch the app store, select the appstore icon from the home screen.

Search & Install

If you are looking for a specific app, such as facebook, the easiest way to install it, is to first search for it using the search field.

To do this tap on the magnifying glass icon on the top right.

In the search field, type the name of the app you want.

To download and install the app, tap the 'download' link next to the app name in the search results.

You'll be able to find all your apps on your home screen. Press the home button at the bottom centre of your screen.

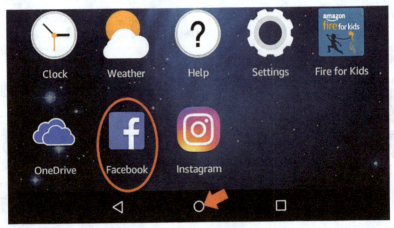

Browse & Install

You can also browse through the categories. From the bar at the top of your screen select the apps category, tap on the 'store' icon, on the far right.

In the app store, you'll see a list of options along the top: 'categories', 'home', 'best sellers', 'underground' and 'for you'.

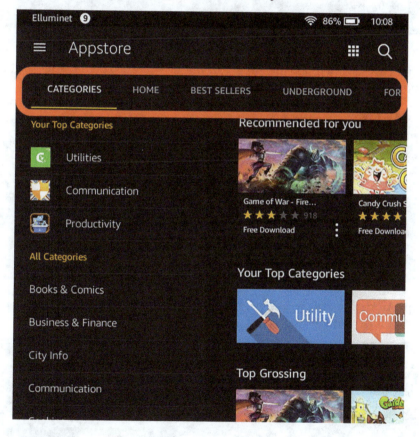

Tap on categories, and you'll see a side bar open up. Scroll down the categories until you find the one you want. In this example, I am going to download an 'office suite', so I'm going to tap 'productivity'.

When you open the category, you'll see a list of the top selling apps in that category, both free apps and paid apps. You'll only be able to see the first two but you can expand the sections if you tap 'see more'.

To see details of the app, just tap on the image.

You'll be able to see details about the app, such as price, reviews and features. To download the app tap on 'download' or the price if it's a paid app - this is the orange button.

Tap on 'download' when prompted. This will download the app and install it on your home screen.

Manage Apps

This allows you to view and manage settings for the apps you've downloaded from the app store. You can uninstall apps, clear app temporary caches, as well as view memory status and storage space. This can be helpful if you are having trouble with a particular app and need to uninstall it or stop it from running.

Swipe down from the top edge of your screen and select settings. Select 'apps and games', then tap 'manage all applications'.

Along the top you'll see some categories. Tap 'downloaded' to view all the apps you've downloaded from the app store. Tap 'running' to see all the apps that are currently running on your Fire Tablet.

To view the app's information, tap on the icon in the list. In this example, I am going to look at the EZCast app.

Here you can force the app to stop, this essentially terminates the app and closes it down - can be useful if the app is not running correctly or has crashed. To do this tap 'force stop'. Tap 'ok' on the confirmation dialog box.

You can also uninstall the app. This is a good thing to do for apps you no longer use as they take up space on your Fire Tablet. To uninstall the app, tap 'uninstall', then tap 'ok' on the confirmation dialog.

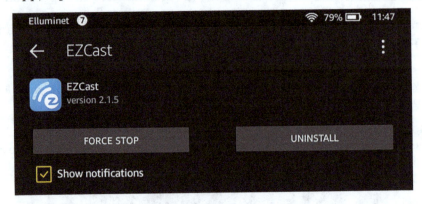

Underneath this you'll see some app stats such as the size of the app (how much space it's taking up), how much data the app has saved to your Fire Tablet, and the size of the cache (temporary files).

It is good practice to periodically clear the data and caches on your apps. This removes temporary files and data that the app saves while it is running. This data isn't really needed and can grow quite large and slow down your Fire Tablet.

To clear the data tap 'clear data', to clear the caches tap 'clear cache'.

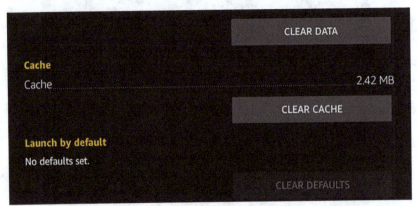

Docs App

If you set up your Amazon Cloud Drive as shown on page 49, you can synchronise documents from your PC to your Fire Tablet. For example, you can synchronise Microsoft Word documents and edit them using your Fire Tablet. To do this, on your PC, open file explorer.

Drag and drop the files you want to work on to 'amazon drive' on the left hand side

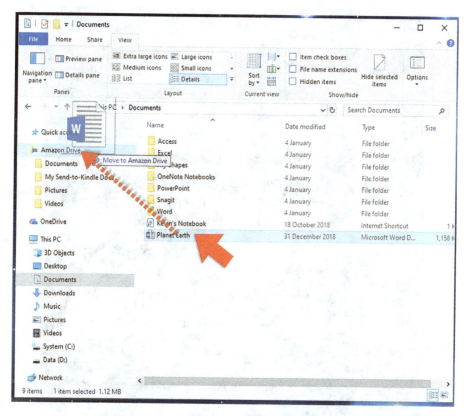

These files will be synchronised to your amazon cloud drive. You'll be able to edit these documents using the docs app on your Fire Tablet.

Note that not all files are compatible with the Fire Tablet and some might not work.

Chapter 5: Using Fire Apps

On your Fire Tablet, select 'home' from the carousel menu along the top of your screen

Tap on the docs app.

When the docs app opens, you'll see files and folders on your fire tablet as well as on your cloud drive. Along the top of the app you'll see your icons for creating, sorting, or selecting documents. The docs app is also split into three sections: 'send-to-kindle', 'cloud drive', and 'local storage'.

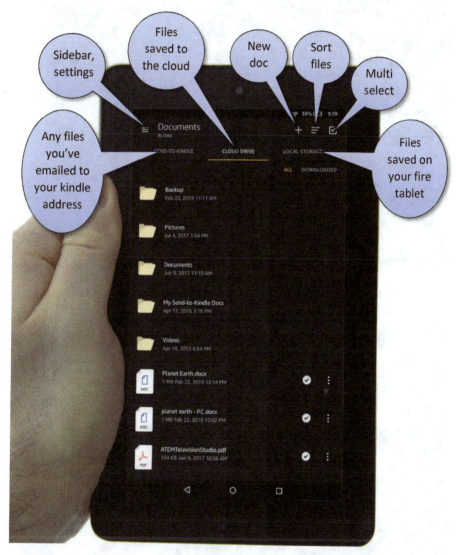

These three sections allow you to view files you have sent using your kindle fire email address, files you've saved onto your amazon cloud drive, and files you have downloaded to your kindle. Just tap on each of the three options to see the files.

In the main section of the app, you'll see all the files and folders listed.

Reading & Editing Documents

Tap on 'cloud drive' on the top of the screen.

Scroll down and select the document you just copied to amazon cloud drive on your PC.

The document will open in 'reading view'. To edit the document, tap the icon in the top right hand corner of the screen.

You'll see a simplified word processor where you can edit your document

New Documents

To create a new document, first select where you want the document to be stored - select 'cloud drive'.

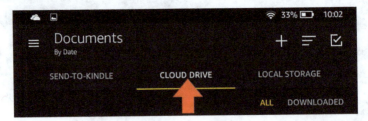

Tap the '+' sign on the top right of the screen, then from the drop down, select the type of document you want: word processing document, spreadsheet or presentation.

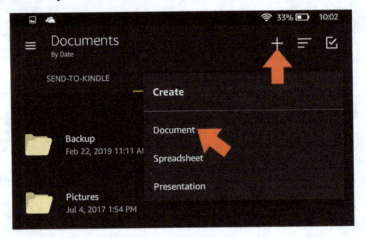

Now you can work on your document.

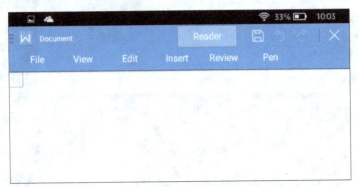

Remember to save your document, tap the 'file' menu, hit the 'save as' icon, then give your document a name.

Sending Files to Fire Tablet

You can send files to your fire tablet using email. To do this, first you need to find out what your fire email address is. Open your settings app, then select 'my account'.

At the top of the screen you'll see an email address. This is the email address you can use to send files to your fire tablet.

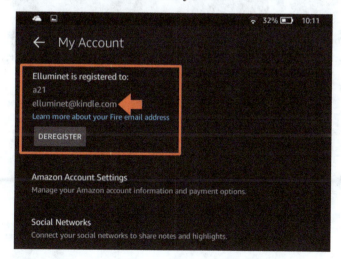

Chapter 5: Using Fire Apps

Now, on your computer or laptop you can use your usual email program to send files to your fire address. Enter your fire email address in the 'to' field, attach a file, then click 'send'.

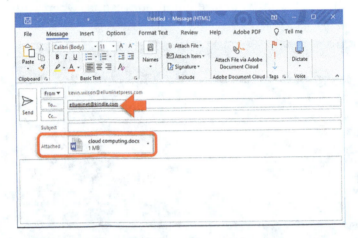

Open your docs app, then select 'send-to-kindle' from the three options along the top of the screen.

You'll see the new document at the top of the list, tap on it to open it up.

Sending Files from Windows File Explorer

You can easily send files to your kindle directly from windows file explorer. Send to Kindle will appear when you right click on a file in windows file explorer or in the print dialog box of any windows application. This is useful if you want to send a PDF or Word document to your kindle, so you can read it on the go.

To get started, first you need to install the 'send to kindle' plugin. On your PC, open your web browser and navigate to:

`www.amazon.com/gp/sendtokindle/pc`

Click 'download now' at the top of the page.

Click 'run' when prompted by your browser, or click the download on the bottom left of the screen.

To send a file to your fire tablet, open windows file explorer.

Navigate to the file you want to send. Right click on the file, then select 'send to kindle'.

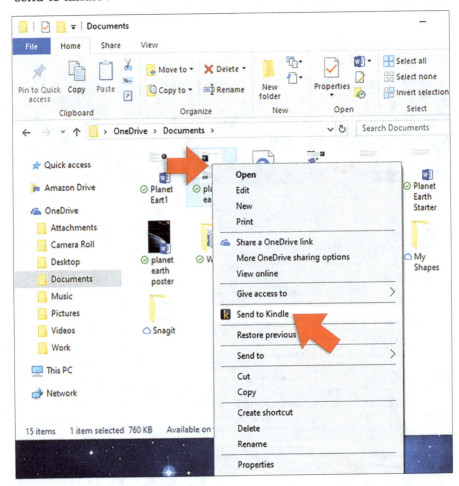

To select more than one file, hold down the control key on your keyboard, then click the files you want to send to highlight them. Right click on the selection, then select 'send to kindle'.

From the dialog box that appears, select the fire tablet you want to send the file to.

Click 'send'.

On your fire tablet, you'll be able to find your file in the docs app. In the docs app, tap 'send to kindle' on the top left.

Tap on the file to open it.

Copy Files to Fire Tablet from PC

You can copy files directly onto your fire tablet from your PC. To do this you will need to plug your fire tablet into your PC using the USB cable.

You'll see your fire tablet appear under the 'this pc' section of windows file explorer.

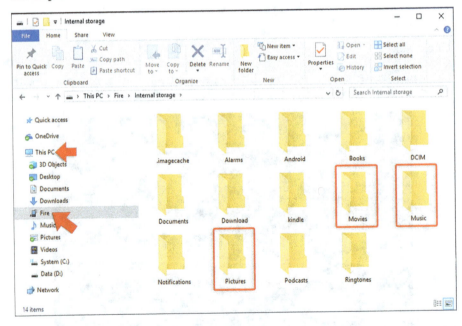

If you want to copy music, drag and drop the music files to the 'music' folder. Similarly if you want to copy over some photos, drag and drop them to the 'pictures' folder.

Clock App

The clock app doesn't just tell the time, it can tell the time in different countries around the world, set timers, alarms and countdowns. To open your clock app, tap the clock icon on the home screen.

When the app opens you'll see the app's main screen. Let's take a look at the different features.

You can set alarms to remind you of something or as a morning wake up call.

You can set world clocks to tell what time it is in other countries.

Countdown timers are useful for timing something. Perhaps you're baking a cake, or cooking something in the oven and it has to cook for a set amount of time, such as 30 minutes.

Stop watch timers are useful to time how long something takes.

You can switch between these four features using the four icons across the top of the screen.

Alarms

To set an alarm, tap the 'alarms' icon on the top left, then tap the '+' icon at the bottom of the screen.

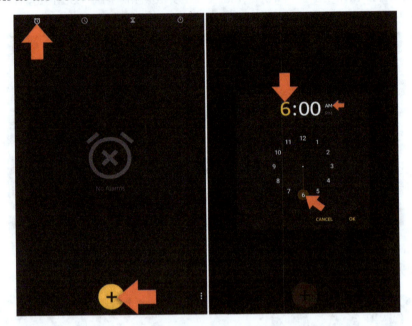

Enter the time you want the alarm to sound. Eg 6:00AM. Tap on the hour (eg 6), then tap the minutes (say if you wanted 10 minutes past, or half past). Tap on 'am' if you want the alarm to sound in the morning, select 'pm' for the evening. Tap 'ok'.

If you want the alarm to sound on different days, tap 'repeat' and select the days you want the alarm on. Eg M, T, W, T, F, and off on S and S.

Tap the 'bell' icon and select an alarm tone. Don't forget to turn the volume to max on your fire tablet so you can hear the alarm clearly.

Use the orange slider on the top right to turn the alarm on or off. Tap the white trash can on the bottom left to delete the alarm.

Clocks

To add a clock for a particular city in a country, select the 'clock' icon from the four icons along the top of the screen. Then tap the orange 'world' icon on the bottom.

From the list, tap on the countries you want to know the time for. Tap the back arrow on the top left to return to the clock app.

To remove a city, tap the 'world' icon on the bottom of the screen, then scroll through the list and untick the clocks you don't want.

Countdown

To start a countdown, tap the countdown icon from the four icons along the top of the screen. Enter the hours, minutes, and seconds for the length of time you want. Eg tap 2 0 then tap 0 0 for 20 minutes.

Hit the 'play' icon at the bottom to start the countdown.

Stopwatch

To time something to see how long it takes, tap the stop watch icon from the list of four icons along the top of the screen

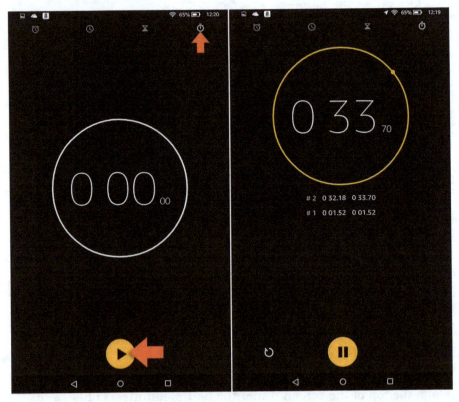

Tap the 'play' icon to start the timer. Tap the icon on the left to set a lap time, if you are timing a race

To stop the timer, tap the pause icon.

To reset the timer, first pause the timer, then tap the icon on the left of the play icon.

You can also share the times using the share icon on the bottom right. First pause the timer, the icon will appear on the right, tap then select the application you want to use to share the times. Eg facebook, or email.

Weather App

The weather app will show you a weather forecast for your current location. To start the weather app, tap the app on your home screen

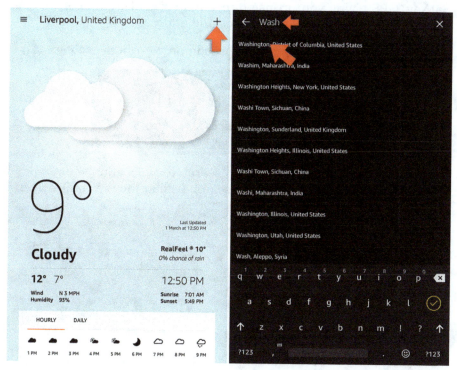

Scroll down the forecast to see the details. If you want to see what the weather is like in another city or country - perhaps you're planning a vacation/holiday. Tap the '+' icon on the top right, then type in the city or country.

To see all the cities/countries you have a weather forecast for, tap the hamburger icon on the top left.

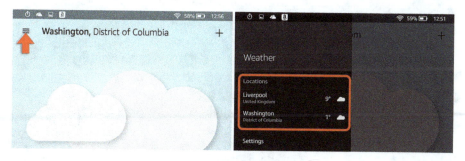

Select the city from the list on the slideout panel.

Maps App

Maps is an extremely useful app if you are trying to find out where a particular place is and need to find driving directions. It works like a SatNav/GPS giving you precise directions straight from door to door. You can also explore different places and addresses.

To start the maps app, tap the maps icon on your home screen.

Once the maps app opens, you can search for a location - just type in an address, or place name into the search field at the top of the screen..

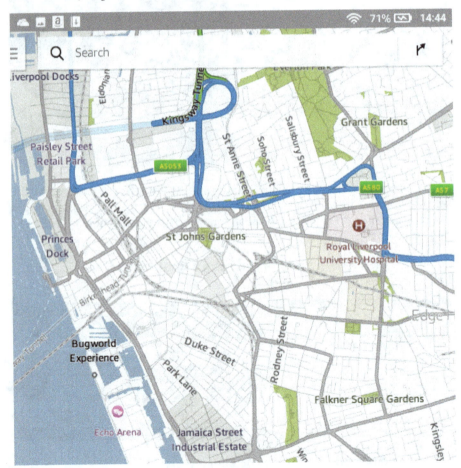

Swipe from the left edge of the screen to open the side panel.

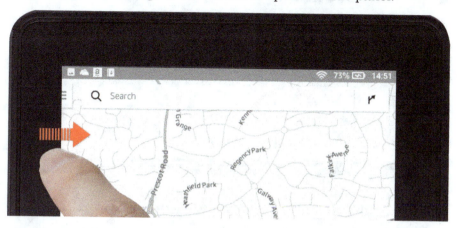

From here you can change the map type. Tap 'satellite' to switch to a satellite map, tap 'traffic' to add traffic stats to the roads.

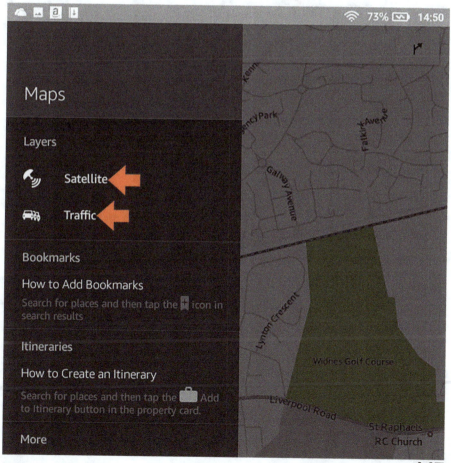

Exploring Locations

Type in an address, city name or placename into the search field at the top of the screen.

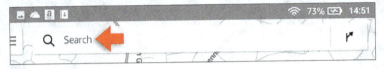

Select an option from the suggestions

You'll see a place card with a map and some details

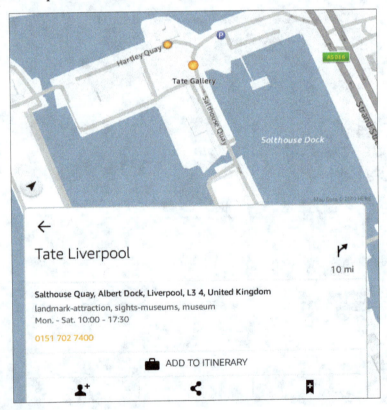

Directions

To get directions to a specific place, tap the directions icon on the top right of the search field.

Along the top of the directions window you'll see a mode of transport: car, public transport and walking.

Next one down is 'route options'. Here you can tell the maps app to avoid toll roads, ferries, motorways/highways, or carpool lanes.

Underneath you can configure your route. The maps app will automatically find your current location, so all you need to do is enter the address of your destination.

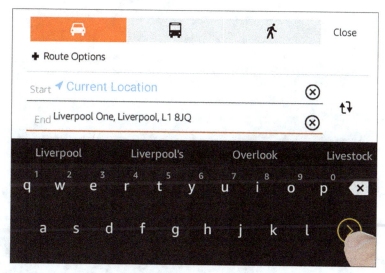

Tap enter on the on-screen keyboard.

149

Chapter 5: Using Fire Apps

The maps app will show a route marked out on a map with an ETA and distance from your current location.

Tap the hamburger icon on the top right to see a list of directions.

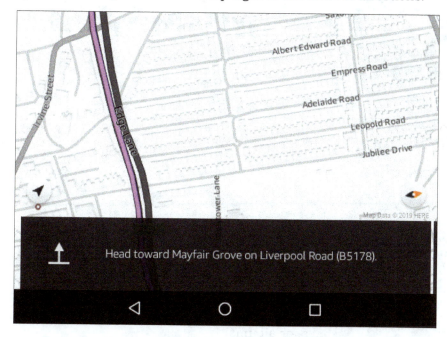

Tap 'preview' on the bottom right to see the route.

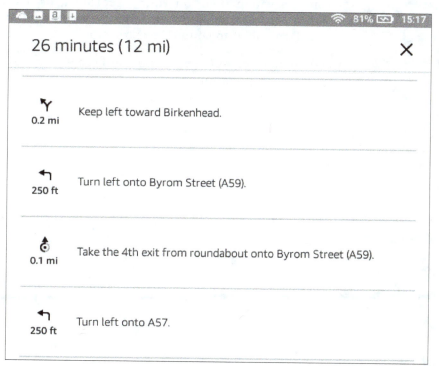

Entertainment

You can watch videos and films you get from Amazon using an Amazon Prime subscription.

If you don't have a subscription to Amazon Prime, you can still buy the individual videos, programmes songs, or albums.

You can watch them on your Fire Tablet, or if you prefer a more cinematic experience, you can hook up your Fire Tablet to your TV or projector.

Lets take a look at the video app and see what videos, films and tv programmes we can find.

Prime Video App

To start the prime video app, tap on the video icon on your home screen.

Browse the Categories

When you launch the app, you'll see some of the latest movies and tv shows that are currently available. Along the top you'll see some categories: 'home', 'originals', 'tv shows', 'movies', and 'kids'.

Here you'll be able to download your favourite tv shows, movies and programmes for kids.

Select a category and browse through the offerings. In this example, I am going to rent a movie. So tap on the 'movies' category.

Anything with the 'prime' logo on, you can watch as part of your amazon prime subscription without paying any extra. If you don't have amazon prime, you can still download the programme but you'll need to pay the fee.

Chapter 6: Entertainment

On the first page, you'll see the top grossing or most popular films, split into groups such as popular films, highest rated, new and recently added and so on, to see more in that particular group tap 'see more' on the right hand side.

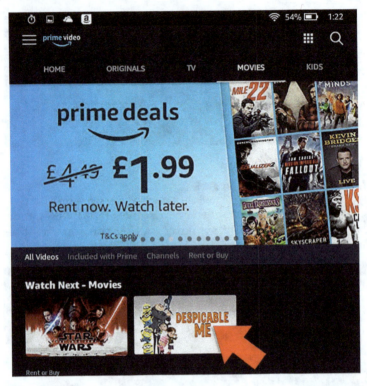

To see more details about a particular programme or film, tap on the thumbnail. This will open up the details section of that particular film or programme.

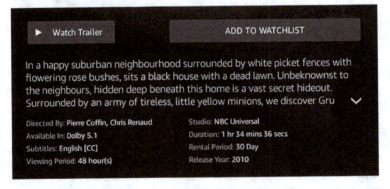

Tap on 'watch trailer' to see the official trailer for the film, or you can tap 'add to watch list' to watch it later.

To buy/rent the film, tap on either 'buy movie...' or 'rent movie...' If you buy the film you can keep it and watch it anytime you like, it's like buying the film on DVD except the film downloads directly to your Fire Tablet and doesn't come on a disc.

If you rent the film you can keep it for 30 days before it is removed automatically from your device, however if you have started watching the film, you'll have 48 hours to finish. In the example, I'm going to rent this movie, so I'm going to tap 'rent movie SD £2.49'.

Once your film is ready, tap on 'watch now'. If you tap 'watch now', the movie will stream over the internet to your device, so this means you'll need a good internet connection.

Searching for TV programmes and Movies

You can also search for your favourite TV programmes or movies. To do this, open up the videos app, then tap the magnifying glass icon on the top right of the screen.

Start typing in the title of the film or TV programme. The Videos App will start displaying possible titles, so if you see the one you want, tap on the name.

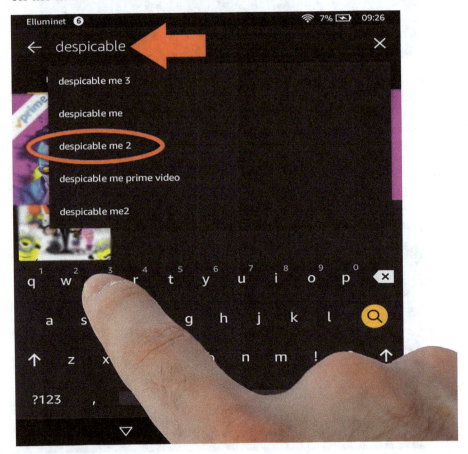

Hook up to a TV

If you have a 'Smart TV', go into your settings and select 'screen share'. This example uses an LG Smart TV, you may need to consult the instructions that came with your TV to find the exact procedure.

Remember the name of your TV, circled below, for when you mirror your fire tablet display to your TV.

From your Fire Tablet, select the settings app from your home screen.

Tap 'display & sounds' and then tap 'display mirroring' - you might not see this option on older fire tablets. Your tablet will search for devices in range. If you're using your smart TV, look for the name of the TV you saw in the previous step and tap on that.

If you're mirroring to your Fire TV Stick, select your TV stick from the options.

When your device connects, you'll be able to see a duplicate of your Fire Tablet's screen on your TV. You can start any app. In this example, I am going to watch a film.

Start the movies app from the home screen to watch your movie.

Whatever you see on your Fire Tablet, you'll see on your TV.

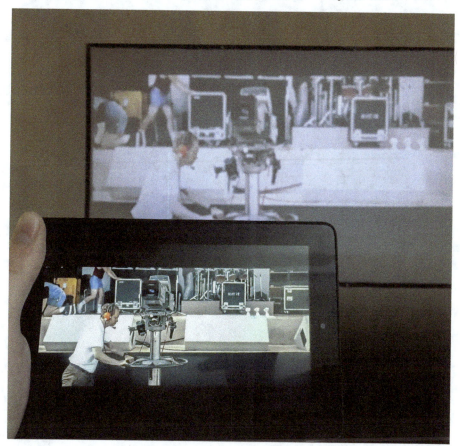

If you have a Fire TV stick, you can mirror your tablet's screen to your stick.

To stop displaying the screen, swipe down from the top of the screen, go to 'display' then 'display mirroring' and tap 'stop mirroring'.

Personal Videos

Tap the My Videos app, circled below

All the videos taken with your on board camera will appear in this app.

You can tap on one of the video thumbnails to view the video clip.

Prime Music App

You can find the video app on your home screen.

When you launch the app, you'll see some of the latest singles and albums that are currently available. Along the top you'll see some categories: 'home', 'recommended', 'stations', and 'playlists'. Lets take a closer look.

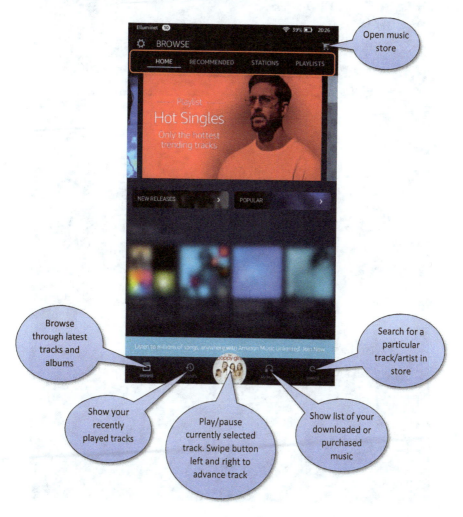

Music Store

You can find the music store in the Music App. To open the store, tap the shopping cart icon on the top right of your screen.

The Music App will display best selling songs and albums, just tap on the album cover or the song to view details.

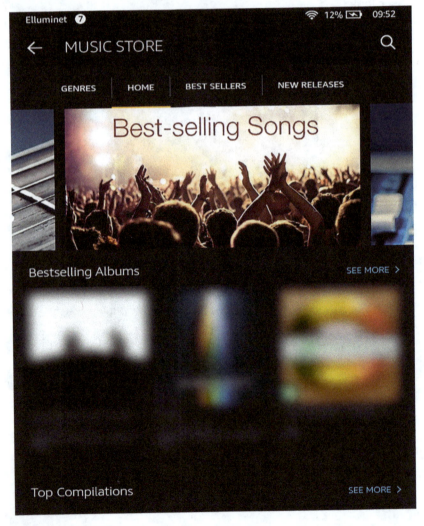

You can also search for your favourite artist, band, or song name. To do this click the magnifying glass icon on the top right of the screen.

Start typing in the name and the Music App will display some possible matches. If you see what you're looking for in the list, tap on the name.

In the search results, you'll see a list of the most popular songs and albums for your keywords.

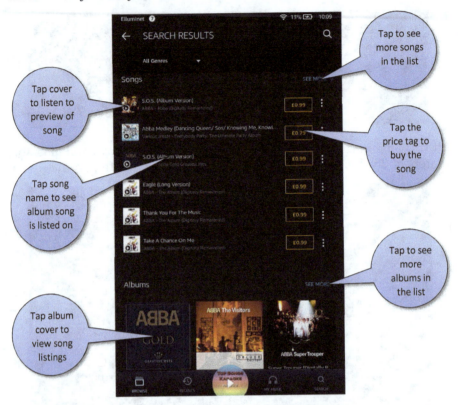

Tap cover to listen to preview of song

Tap to see more songs in the list

Tap song name to see album song is listed on

Tap the price tag to buy the song

Tap to see more albums in the list

Tap album cover to view song listings

If you have Amazon Prime you can stream the full recordings of these tracks and albums without having to buy the individual tracks.

Streaming Music

With Prime Music, you have access to two million songs. If you want something to pass the time with, and love listening to the great classics in any genre, this option is perfect. This option is included with an Amazon Prime subscription.

If you like keeping up with the latest bands, artists, and releases, it's worth signing up for Amazon Music Unlimited. This service has fifty million songs, and includes new albums, and artists.

Newer artists is where you'll notice the largest difference between the two plans. To sign up open your web browser and navigate to:

www.amazon.com/AmazonMusicUnlimited

Playing your Music

Your Fire Tablet has on-board speakers, the smaller tablets only have one speaker and isn't particularly good quality. The HD Fire Tablets have stereo speakers and are a little better. To improve the sound quality, you can connect headphones or external speakers to the 3.5mm (1/8th inch) jack on the top of your Fire Tablet.

To find your purchased/downloaded music, tap, 'my music' on the bottom of the screen.

Chapter 6: Entertainment

To play a track, tap on one in the list.

Volume controls are on the top of your Fire Tablet.

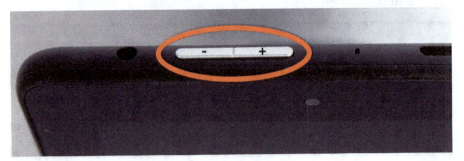

When you tap on a track, you'll see the album/track cover and some controls down at the bottom of the screen.

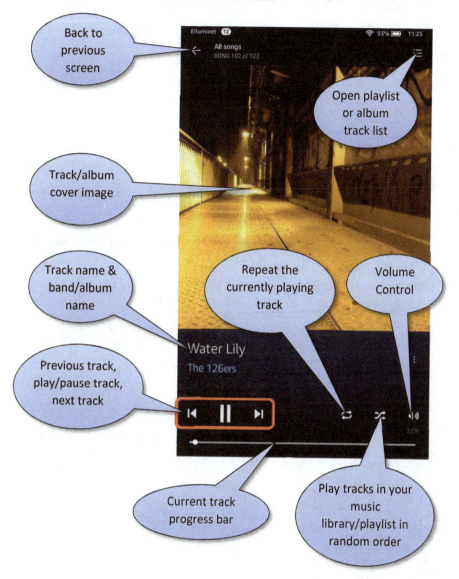

Back to previous screen

Open playlist or album track list

Track/album cover image

Track name & band/album name

Repeat the currently playing track

Volume Control

Previous track, play/pause track, next track

Current track progress bar

Play tracks in your music library/playlist in random order

Books and Magazines

With the Amazon Fire Tablet, you have access to thousands of kindle books and magazines.

You can read your favourite stories, genres, as well as text books and other non-fiction.

You can either purchase the book and keep it in your library, or you can borrow from the kindle lending library if you have an Amazon Prime or Kindle Unlimited membership.

You can purchase magazine or newspaper subscriptions or buy individual issues if you prefer. These are all downloaded directly to your newsstand on your newsstand app.

Kindle Books

You'll find all your kindle books on the Kindle Books App.

When you start the app, you'll see the main screen. From here you can see the books you have purchased and downloaded.

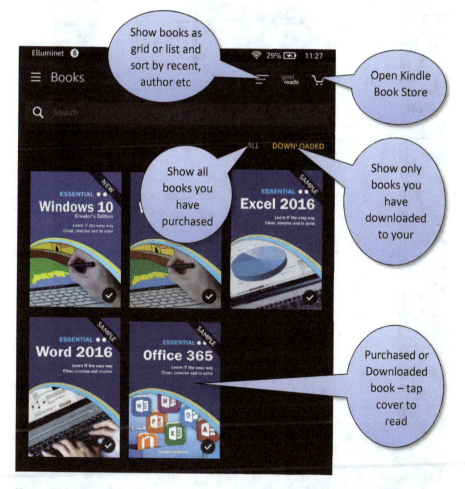

To read a book just tap on the cover. You can also open the kindle store and purchase more books

You can swipe your finger left and right across the screen to turn your pages.

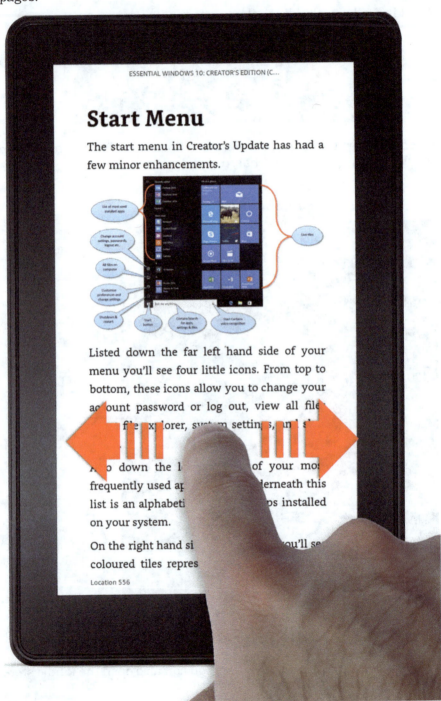

You can also bring up your options. To do this tap your finger anywhere on your screen.

Have a look at the illustration below. Here, you can open the book's table of contents, and jump to any section, you can change the screen font size, add book mark to the current page, as well as adding your own notes to the pages. Just tap on the icons.

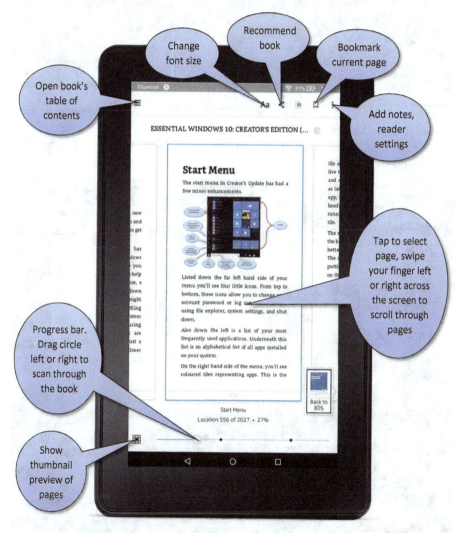

When you're finished reading, tap the back arrow on the bottom left of your screen to go back to your book library screen.

Kindle Store

If you want to browse the book store, from the main screen tap the store icon on the top right of the book library screen.

You'll see a list of recommended and best selling books. To view or buy any of the books you see, just tap on the cover. You can also search for authors, titles or genres. To do this type your keywords into the search field indicated below.

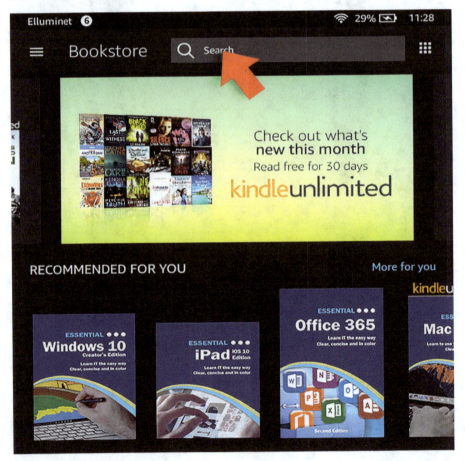

The kindle store will return a list of books according to your search terms. In this example I am searching for Windows 10 books.

To view the book details tap on the book's front cover.

You can view a sample of the book. Tap 'download sample'. This will download the first 10% of the book. If you like the book tap 'buy now' to buy the book.

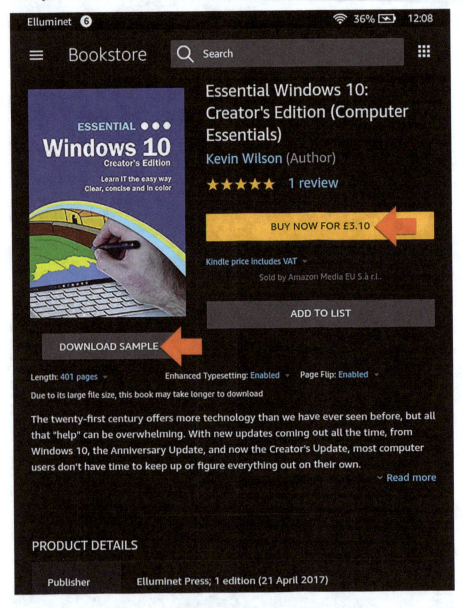

You can also see a description of the book, customer reviews and some technical stats on the book such as number of 'pages', size in megabytes, book ranking, publisher and ISBN details.

The book will be downloaded and added to your book library.

Newsstand

As well as reading books, you can also read newspapers and magazines. You'll find these in the newsstand app.

If you haven't downloaded any magazines, tap 'shop in newsstand', or tap the shopping cart icon on the top right.

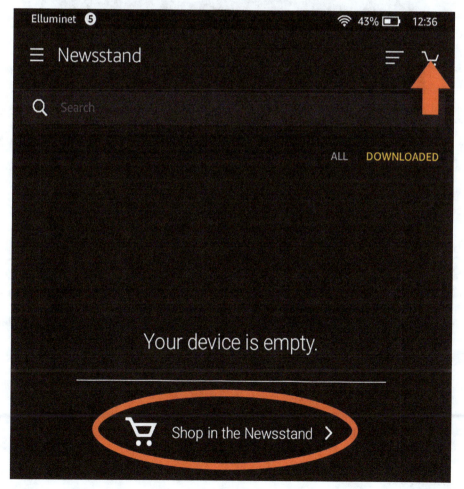

Chapter 7: Books and Magazines

This will take you to the store. Here you'll see a list of popular magazines in some of the best selling categories such as lifestyle, arts and entertainment and so on.

Tap on any of the covers, to view details. This one on photography seems ok.

Here, you'll see all the details on the magazine. You will see the price. If you go down to purchase options, you can pay the annual subscription, which means you'll receive a new edition each month, or you can just purchase the current issue, if you just want a one off.

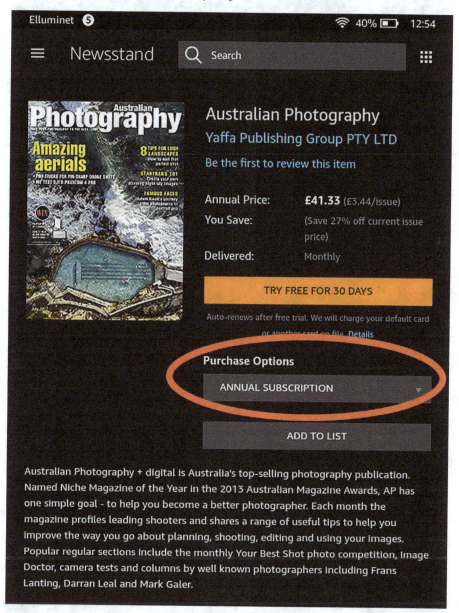

Further down, you can read a product description telling you about what to expect from the magazine, as well as some technical stats such as size in megabytes, number of pages, publisher information etc.

Once you've downloaded your magazine, you'll find it in your news stand.

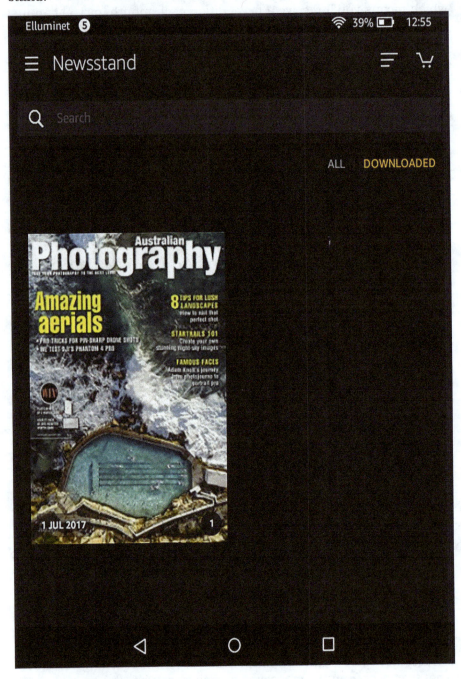

Tap on the magazine cover to open it up

When your magazine opens up, you can start to read. Swipe your finger left or right across the screen to turn the pages. To open up the options bar at the top, tap in the centre of the screen.

From here you can open up the table of contents and jump to any page in the magazine, you can display all the pages as thumbnails so you can quickly find what you're looking for. You can also bookmark pages so you can get back to parts of the magazine quickly.

You can enable reader view. This is black text on a white background and removes the column formatting making it easier to read, as shown below.

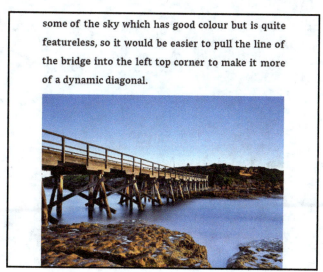

You can also read the daily newspapers. From the newsstand store, tap on 'all newspapers'

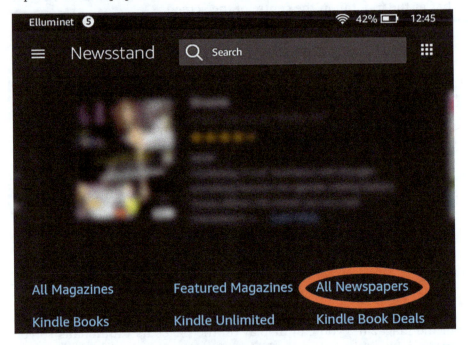

You'll see a list of current newspapers according to your region. Tap on any of the covers to open up the details of the newspaper.

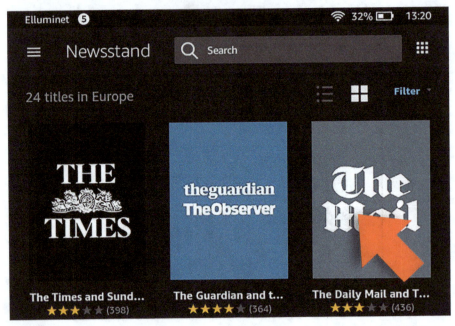

Here you'll see price details, you can either pay a subscription and get a new edition each time it's published, or you can just buy a one off copy. To do this go down to purchase options and change between 'monthly subscription' or 'current issue'.

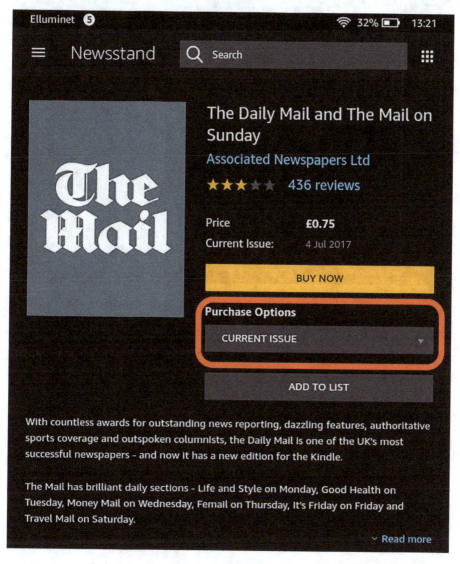

To download the newspaper, tap on 'buy now'.

Chapter 7: Books and Magazines

Your newspaper will appear in your newsstand.

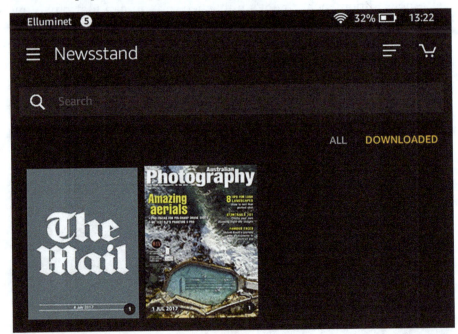

Tap on the thumbnail cover to open it up to read. When your newspaper opens up, you can start to read. Swipe your finger left or right across the screen to turn the pages. To open up the options bar at the top, tap in the centre of the screen.

Tap the icon on the top left to open up the table of contents.

From here you can scan through the headlines and articles that interest you in your newspaper. Tap on the article in the list to jump to that page.

Tap the back arrow at the bottom left to return to your newsstand.

Cameras and Photos

Your Fire Tablet has two cameras; one at the back and one at the front. You can take photos or shoot videos, edit them and post them to your friends.

You can also import photos from memory cards, flash drives or directly from your camera.

Lets take a look around the Photos App.

Prime Photos App

You will find the Prime Photos App, on your home screen.

When the app starts, you'll see all the photos you have taken with your Fire Tablet's camera. Lets take a closer look at the screen.

Edit a Photo

To edit a photo, tap on the photo from the main screen to open it. Now tap the '3 dots' icon on the top right.

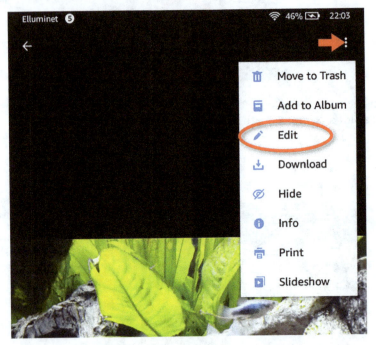

From the drop down menu, tap 'edit'.

Along the bottom of the screen you'll see a list of effects and tools. You can add frames, funny stickers, brightness, contrast, text and drawing tools. In this example, I'm going to change the brightness of this photograph. So, tap the brightness icon.

Along the bottom of the screen you'll see some options. With the brightness option, you can adjust the overall exposure of the photograph. 'Contrast' adjusts the difference between light and dark parts of the photo. 'Highlights' adjusts only the bright parts of the photo. 'Shadows' adjusts only the dark parts of the photo - useful if you want to lighten a part of your photo that is in shadow.

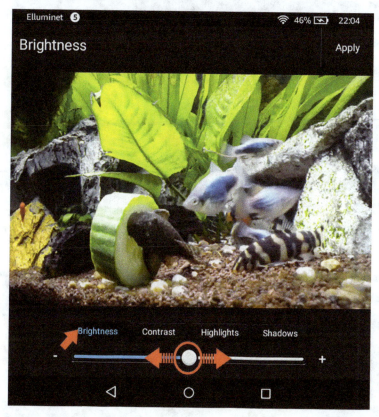

To make the adjustment, tap the option, in this example I'm adjusting the brightness, so I'll choose 'brightness'.

Then drag the slider to the right to increase the brightness, and to the left to reduce the brightness. Do the same with contrast, highlights and shadows. Try experimenting with some of the other effects.

How about adding a frame? Or some amusing stickers? Give it a try.

Share a Photo

Tap on the photo you want to share from your main screen. This will open it up in edit mode. In this example, I want to share the photo we were just editing on facebook.

From edit mode, tap 'share' on the top right of the screen.

Next, select where you want to share the photo. In this example, I am posting to facebook, but you could email it.

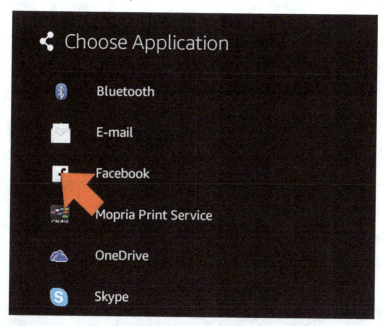

You may be prompted for your facebook username and password, enter them in the dialog if prompted.

Type your caption on the right hand side, then tap 'post' when you're done.

Camera App

You will find the Camera App on your home screen

Once the app opens, you'll see an image from the rear camera. Lets take a look at some of the options.

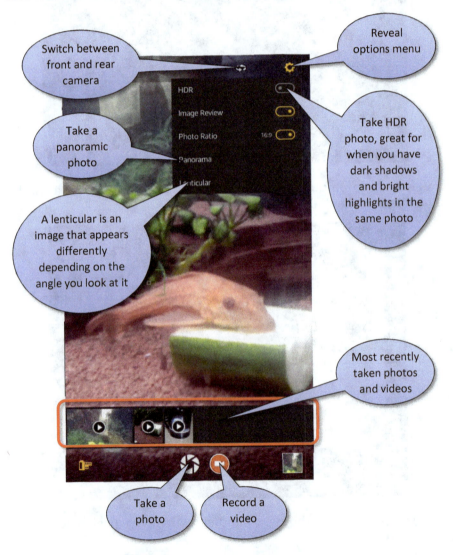

Taking Photos & Recording Video

Tap on the image on the screen to set your focus.

Pinch the screen with your forefinger and thumb to zoom in and out.

Chapter 8: Cameras and Photos

To take your photograph, tap on the shutter icon, at the bottom centre of the screen. If you want to record a video, tap the red camcorder icon next to the shutter icon.

Panoramic Photos

Tap the cog icon on the top right, then select 'panoramic' from the drop down.

Hold your Fire Tablet up then tap the blue button at the bottom to begin shooting your panorama.

Now slowly pan your tablet to the right. As you do this, you'll see a rectangular image appear in the centre.

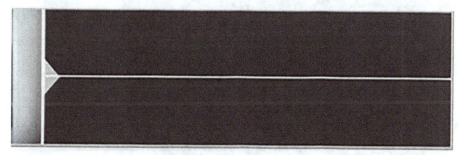

This is a preview of the panoramic image. Keep panning your Fire Tablet. When you've taken enough of the scene, tap the blue button again to finish.

Photo Importer

You can import photos from a flash drive, micro SD card, using the card slot on the side, or directly from your camera using a micro USB OTG cable.

An OTG Cable (USB On-The-Go), allows your Fire Tablet to act as a host, allowing your digital camera to be attached to it. Plug your USB flash drive or USB cable from your camera into the standard USB end of the OTG cable. Plug the micro USB end into your Fire Tablet.

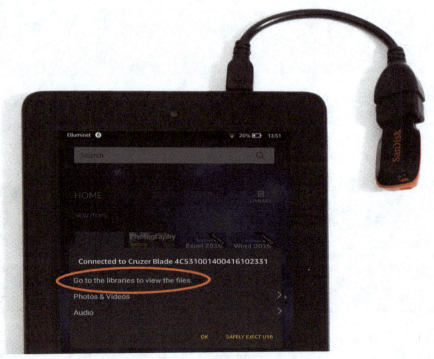

Tap 'go to the libraries to view the files', when prompted.

You'll see your photos appear in the Prime Photos App. Note that these photos have not been imported, you are just seeing what is on the camera/flash drive.

To import the photos, tap and hold your finger on one of the photos. You'll see a blue bar appear along the top of the screen. Now tap on the rest of the photos, you'll see a blue border appear around each photo you select.

Once you have done that, tap the upload icon on the blue bar on the top right. This will upload the photos to your amazon cloud and they will appear in Prime Photos App when you disconnect your camera / flash drive

You can also plug your camera in using the OTG cable. Just plug the micro USB from your camera into the standard USB end of the OTG cable.

Tap the tick icon on the top right of the screen to import the photos (indicated with red arrow above). Tap the photos you want to import.

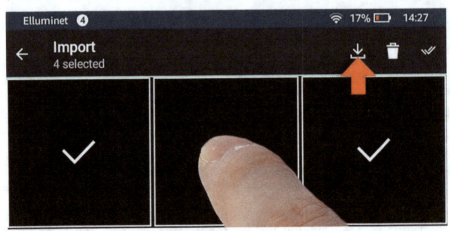

Then tap the import icon on the right hand side (indicated with red arrow above).

Give your album a name in the field indicated with the red arrow below.

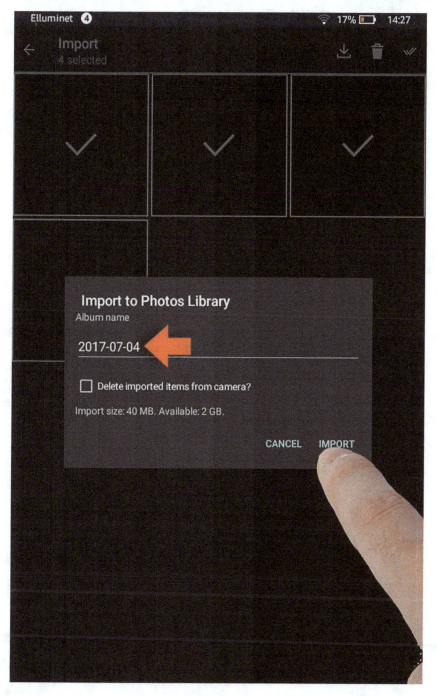

Then tap 'import' to import the photographs into Prime Photos App.

Video Resources

To help you understand the procedures and concepts explored in this book, we have developed some video resources and app demos for you to use as you work through the book.

To find the resources, open your web browser and navigate to the following website

`www.elluminetpress.com/resources/fire-tablets`

At the beginning of each chapter, you'll find a website that contains the resources for that chapter.

When you open the link to the video resources, you'll see a thumbnail list at the bottom.

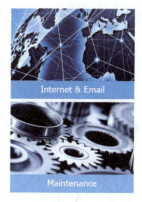

Click on the thumbnail for the particular video you want to watch. Most videos are between 30 and 60 seconds outlining the procedure, others are a bit longer.

When the video is playing, hover your mouse over the video and you'll see some controls...

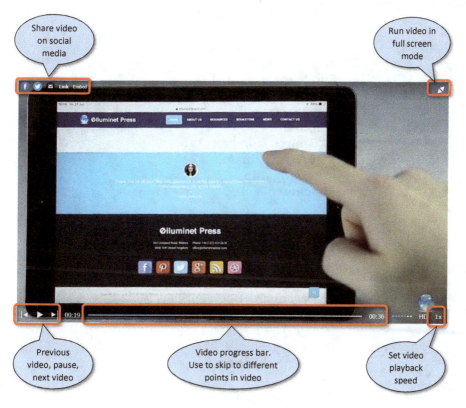

Index

C

D

E

F

G

Index

H

I

K

M

N

P

Index

www.ingramcontent.com/pod-product-compliance
Lightning Source LLC
LaVergne TN
LVHW012330060326
832902LV00011B/1801